MOMENTUM
MAKERS

100 SOCIAL MEDIA TIPS FROM TOP PRODUCING NETWORK MARKETERS

A NETWORK MARKETING BOOK BY
BEACH MONEY PUBLICATIONS

Beach Money
PUBLICATIONS

D1606885

Published by Beach Money Publications
9885 Wyecliff Drive, Suite 200
Highlands Ranch, CO 80126
BeachMoneyPublications.com

Contributing Authors:
Allison Luckadoo, Laura Caroffino, Jessica Hefley, Andrew Eaton, Codi Bills, Jessie Welte, Mallory Garshnick, Jennifer Boucher, Nichole Smith, Julia Lane Cooper, Erica Anderson, Craig Schulze, Amber Spence, Nici Hinkel, Shawn & Michelle Poe, Jessica Menard, Jody Chase, Christina Watts, Amanda Arnett, Brian Fryer, DJ Barton

Manufactured in the United States of America.

ISBN: 978-1-62865-806-4

TESTIMONIALS —
MAXIMIZE YOUR SUCCESS

What Jordan Adler and his co-authors have put together in this book is pretty awesome. To have a book filled with social media tips and strategies from different viewpoints and levels of success is immensely valuable. I have been a Jordan Adler fan ever since I met him, and he knows how to bring value in an incredible way! This book will help you and your team become better at navigating the social media landscape!

Ray Higdon
Founder of RankMakers and co-author of *Freakishly Effective Social Media for Network Marketers*

This book takes you behind the scenes with network marketers who have already gone where you want to go. You'll get to hear their stories and learn their practical strategies that produce results! Momentum Makers is a must read for anyone building a network marketing business online. You must have a social media strategy if you want to succeed in today's business landscape.

Adrian Chenault
Founder, Contact Mapping

Wow! Simply wow! The depth and knowledge of all the authors in this book about building my MLM business using social media is priceless. I now have a better understanding of how to plan my posts, utilize my time, and build my brand, which is really just being my authentic self and building relationships with others on social media.

Katrena Card
Plainfield, IL

I love this book! It's like having a 1:1 training seminar with seasoned experts, minus the crowds and uncomfortable seats! Practical, down to earth, real, and raw examples of how network marketing can change your life if you want it to.

Jaime Williams
Jerome, AZ

Couple pretty emotional stories. That is a staggering collection of testimonials and probably the greatest book I've ever read on this industry next to Beach Money, and I am not blowing smoke up your butt. LOL

Trevor Walsh
Olalla, WA

Contents

FOREWORD

For several years now, I've been bringing you books that focus on the soft skills necessary for success in the network marketing industry. These soft skills are beneficial in almost every industry, but they are the skills that can truly make or break a network marketer. They are the skills that would be most often identified in people who are known to be charismatic—the people that others are drawn to—the people that others WANT to work with.

But this isn't that type of book.

No, this book isn't going to focus on those soft skills again . . .

This book will take it a step further giving you real, applicable examples that will allow you to INCORPORATE those soft skills into your use of various social media platforms.

Why?

Let me explain.

This book will take you out of the learning phase of your personal/ professional development and transition you into the application phase!! It will give real life examples of how industry leaders have created momentum using these strategies and various social media platforms. You will be able to apply these strategies too.

e with an abundance mindset and firmly believe
t there for everyone who's willing to work for it.
ut success or money, there's always "enough."
not take away from someone's ability to be
person's good fortune does not make it less likely that
else will also have good fortune.

So sharing these PROVEN success strategies just makes sense!

If they work for one person, they CAN work for others, if they are shared with others and implemented correctly. The key to implementing any strategy is this: Make sure it jives with who you truly are. Yes, strategies can be effective, but they will almost always lead to burn out or disappointment if they do not speak to who you are as a person.

Now, I'm not talking about staying in your comfort zone. This doesn't mean that you shouldn't try new things or that, if it doesn't come easy, you shouldn't do it. That's not what I mean.

I'm talking about things that just feel wrong or as though you aren't being genuine or authentic.

If anyone understands this, it's me.

When I started in network marketing, I had so much to learn. And I was a total introvert!! But I was willing to try new things, implement new strategies, and to figure out what worked for ME!

I had to learn how to sell. I had to learn how to network. I had to learn how to recruit. And eventually I became the number one recruiter out of a million distributors!

Maybe you're thinking, "That's great, Rob, but putting myself out there and figuring out social media—it's just too overwhelming. There's too much to learn between Facegram, Instatweet, SnapTube . . . I'll never be able to get a handle on it."

Maybe you understand the social part of social media, but you aren't sure how to use the platforms in an authentic way for your business.

Maybe you already have a following and some success under your belt, and you just aren't sure how to get to the next level.

Whatever your comfort level, whatever your goal, this is the book for you.

Even though I have retired from network marketing, I still coach and help network marketing businesses and people around the world. The best part of my job is being able to help people from any network marketing company learn and implement the skills necessary to create success in this business. And that's exactly what I want for YOU!

So, here's how to best use this book.

Before you start, try to identify three things that you'd like to improve or learn regarding your use of social media for your network marketing business. Jot those three things down. You can use paper, the Notes app on your phone, the target receipt in your purse . . . whatever you have and are most comfortable with. You just want to keep those three things on the forefront.

Then, as you read, make notes in the margin when you come across something that relates to one of the three things that you identified.

You can also make three columns in your notes, one for each of the three areas you'd like to improve, and jot the page numbers down when you come to specific, relevant information about each topic.

Lastly, start small. If you've noted 57 of the 100 tips, jumping and implementing all 57 at the same time would probably be overwhelming and not very effective. Start with one or two. Implement them with fidelity. Practice with them, fine tune them, and get them right!! Then move on to the next one or two on your list.

You don't have to overhaul everything all at once.

Remember, it's a marathon, not a sprint!

JORDAN ADLER

FOREWORD

When Tony Ferraro, my business partner in the Momentum Makers Project reminded me to put together a Foreword to the Social Media Edition, my first thought was, "What do I know about Social Media?" I really don't have that many followers on the platforms so who am I to talk about Social Media? But the truth is, my book Beach Money is all over the world as a result of word of mouth communicated nearly 100% by social media! People post daily about it on Instagram and Facebook. They tweet about it and make YouTube videos about Beach Money and my books. The hashtag #beachmoney didn't exist until my book came out yet that hashtag has been used hundreds of thousands of times. And I sell thousands of books as a result of the Beach Money chatter on social media. So maybe I know a little.

Why should you read this book? Mostly because social media represents the fastest, easiest, and quickest way to communicate, connect, and engage in today's fast-paced world. Which means it represents the shortest distance between you and your dreams. And of course, you are holding in your hands one of the most complete guides to social media being communicated by a group of the most prolific social media experts in network marketing and sales on the planet.

If your parents or grandparents were in network marketing, their worldview on the way the business should be done would have looked quite different than it does today! If they were out driving and needed to make a phone call, they would be searching for a phone booth and then pulling over to a gas station or convenience store. If it was snowing, cold, or rainy, they would need to find an enclosed booth or face the elements. If they weren't in too much of a rush, they might find a nice hotel to make their call. And of course, they had to have change! No change, no call. Until of course calling cards came out! And if the person they were calling wasn't home, their cassette tape answering machine would click on and they would have to leave a message! Getting a call back was tough unless you happened to be home. And when long-distance phone service was .30 per minute, it would not be uncommon for a network marketer with a growing team to rack up phone bills of $2000-$3000 per month! There were no videos . . . only calls and live meetings or events.

If you wanted to present your opportunity to someone, you had to set an appointment, confirm it and meet your prospect at a restaurant or cafe hoping that they didn't cancel or no-show. Of course, you could always invite them to a hotel meeting. If you happened to have a new group pop up in another city, you would be booking your flights, confirming your accommodations, putting together your agenda and volunteers to run the door and set-up. I have flown across the country probably over 100 times to an expected crowd only to find a few seats full.

And let's say they wanted to have a conversation with the top earner or the owner of their company to get some advice or offer feedback. To make that happen, you would need to find out where that top earner was speaking and plan to be there! There would be a crowd of hundreds or thousands of people. When the meeting was complete, you would make your way to the front only to stand in line to get one minute max for a quick photo and handshake or hug. There was no way to call them or even leave a message to have them call or message you back. You had no access to the top money earners or company owners unless you were one of them. Today, you can send a message directly to anyone through virtually any one of the social media platforms and you can be almost 100% sure that that top money earner or even company owner received it.

Today social media allows you to connect with anyone on the planet within seconds. You'll still need to earn their trust and know-how to build relationships. That hasn't changed. It's a noisier world online and grabbing someone's attention takes a little more skill and finesse due to the barrage of communication we get each day.

But thanks to experts like the ones in this book, you'll avoid some of the ugly pitfalls that can cause you to get ignored. You'll need to figure out where your best audience is and with just a few hours of training or just by fumbling around, you'll learn how to navigate any platform. I believe you are better off picking 2-3 platforms to master rather than spreading yourself out over all of them. It's easy to get overwhelmed when you start. Between Facebook, Instagram, LinkedIn, TikTok, Youtube, Snapchat, and all the others, it's easy to get lost in the sea of complexity! But having a plan can help. There are also some simple strategies that you can deploy that will make your life easier and more productive online.

In this book, look for answers to the following questions:

1. Where is my best potential distributor, affiliate, or customer hanging out?

2. When someone goes to my profile, what feeling does it leave them with?

3. How do I engage with a stranger in order to turn them into a relationship?

4. What is my brand and who will it attract?

5. How do I turn a friend into a distributor, affiliate, or customer online?

6. What is my overall social media strategy?

Once you have read this book and have answers to these questions, you will be well prepared to launch your business into a world of endless opportunity! The world wide web gives you access to anyone and anything. You'll expand your reach beyond your wildest dreams.

Jordan Adler
Network Marketing Millionaire
Author of the Amazon Best Sellers *Beach Money* and *Better than Beach Money*
Publisher, Beach Money Publications
Future Astronaut

ALLISON LUCKADOO

ENRICHING RELATIONSHIPS & CONNECTING WITH OTHERS

Salad Dressing. That's what I wanted. Brianna's Blush Vinaigrette. Delicious, gourmet salad dressing. I wanted to be able to buy any salad dressing I wanted, without the budget-friendly lecture that came with it (☺). Don't get me wrong, my husband was just trying to keep our household afloat in a super trying time; but, at the time, I was busy adjusting to life as a "stay-at-home mom" with our two small children after getting laid off from my pharmaceutical sales job in 2009. Talk about a change of plans and a change of lifestyle. "Staying home" was always something I had hoped to do, but since we were trying to build a future and build a nest egg, we had decided that for me to continue to work was optimal, despite the way it tugged at my heart. Ironically enough, those plans were changed, WITHOUT my say so! But like most parents put into difficult and unplanned situations, we figured it out as we went—one day at a time. I chose to look at the shock of losing my job as a window of opportunity to be more active in raising my children, something that was very important to me.

Our new life and budget looked A LOT different once we had two children and one salary. We had to make A LOT of changes. Those changes were worth it, but we found out we just didn't have anything left at the end of month. The budget was just too tight. What we were doing wasn't working anymore. We weren't able to say "yes" to fun activities for the kids, date nights, or things that needed to be fixed around the house without going into debt! Honestly, being overly stressed with finances was becoming the new "norm." Cue the infamous "budget discussions," which were NOT one of my favorite dinner conversations. It was after one of these dreaded talks one evening in January, after we had spent most of our month's budget for Christmas, that I decided I had to make a change.

I decided to explore my options. I sent out a few resumes for the "typical" 9-5 job, but I was already feeling the longing of wanting to still be able to pick up my babies from their naps and snuggle their sweet little bodies. I decided to pay attention to a few "God-given" signs and listen to a friend who had reached out to me regarding a network marketing opportunity that was making waves in the skin-care industry.

Now, mind you, this was something I NEVER saw myself doing. I didn't think this type of business was something someone could "actually" succeed in. But after doing a little research, I realized this was a solid company, backed by still practicing doctors and a powerful brand. When paired with the newly budding social commerce channel, I would be able to share it with everyone I was connected to electronically. It was a no-brainer. Better yet, due to the flexibility of this incredible platform, I knew that I was going to be able to have the same impact as a mother as I could have as a business owner. The ability to build a business, from home, from the palm of my hand, around my children? Yep, this was worth giving a try. I realized though I was thinking outside the box and that not everyone was going to grasp this new, non-traditional way of doing business. But I knew this was an avenue worth exploring. After all, what did I have to lose? I felt like I had been given a gift, and I wanted to share it with everyone! So I got to work.

I excelled once I took advantage of this powerful opportunity. I was promoted to the top level of our company in three years and have maintained that level for the past four consecutive years. Furthermore, I was able to earn a company car in just over two years.

My family's life financially is completely unrecognizable from what it was in 2013, and I was able to do it on my terms. How did I do it? I used my drive, talent, networking skills, social network, and education to build MY business the way I wanted to. Combining my company and its stellar products with a very powerful social media platform became an avenue to change my life and the lives of others.

Just because network marketing is a simple concept, it certainly does not mean that it is easy. However, it is POWERFUL, if you are willing to take the time to learn the process and best practices. I soaked up advice from those who had experienced success in running network-marketing businesses. I read books on this business model and this industry. I studied social media trends. I tried things that failed, then tweaked them until they succeeded.

How did I do it? I got connected. I utilized a platform that was FREE and that allowed me to develop and maintain relationships of every kind. Gone were the days of business cards; I now had a social highway to make new connections and discover ways that I could help my network meet a need and add value to their lives. My new business card was "What's your Insta handle?" or "Can I find you on Facebook?" Then, I let them know I would be following up and/or I would love to get to know them better! Having enriching relationships and connecting with others has always been a passion of mine: this is what I built the foundation of my business on.

When starting any type of business, I believe you have to fall in love with what you are doing and how it can help your friends. That is where you anchor your goals. If it's all about the money or gaining the most success, that will only get you so far. And NEWS FLASH: it certainly won't help you get through the hard times when that bottom line doesn't always match with your goals.

3 Key Aspects of how I built my successful business utilizing social media are as follows:

1. Positive Team Culture

2. The Art of Utilizing your Network

3. Developing Trust

Let's dig a little deeper in to how social media can assist you in achieving these things and help you reach your goals in your business!

1. Positive Team Culture. When your team excels, you excel. So how can we help them excel? In my business, I have always put my teammates' goals ahead of mine. I believe they have entrusted me with helping them build a business, and I will do everything in my power to assist them as they learn the process. Additionally, keeping your team engaged is a huge aspect of this! So how can we increase engagement and help them feel supported?

Facebook Groups: A method my business has used to connect the team together through social media is by building Facebook Groups. Facebook Groups allowed us to form a type of community/office space for our Consultants. This is a "safe place" where our Consultants can ask questions, recognize special efforts or promotions, and pass along and discuss important strategies or company info.

Team Camaraderie: I developed a Team Name and started recognizing top leaders throughout the month based on various topics including sales numbers, signing business partners, and other fun "awards" for people to shoot for. This has encouraged camaraderie among our team, and by consistently doing this, it has allowed consultants to strive towards these goals every month AND has helped build momentum.

Virtual Events & Groups: We have also formed other groups for special sales or business presentations. With these "Virtual Events," we are able to converse with people all over the globe to discuss our products and the opportunity provided at the time.

Remote One-On-Ones: I have also experienced great success with the Zoom app, which is a virtual meeting room that can connect you with potential clients and prospects.

These options are free, which is a super cost-effective bonus. These options also allow everyone, both Consultant and Prospects, to tune in from their phone. The presentations can also be recorded, so that your prospect can tune in at a time that works for them. These groups have been essential in sharing about our company with others!

2. Utilizing Your Network! Social media has been a GAME CHANGER in this aspect of my business. I honestly believe I would not have been able to reach the success I have with this company without social media. It is the answer to every prospect that says that they are "new in town and don't know a lot of people" or who have had to move a lot with their family or job! This is why social media is BRILLIANT! Because of social media, you now have access to everyone you have ever known ELECTRONICALLY!

Today, almost everyone has a social media account of some sort. I use Facebook and Instagram as a way to connect with new and old friends. Asking to become "friends" on Facebook has become the new "Business Card" for every industry. Connecting with others and adding value to their life is everything.

Facebook Messenger and Instagram have been huge factors in how I start conversations and how I follow up with leads. Following up is CRITICAL! The great thing about the platform is that it is free and takes all of the stress out of introducing yourself.

Sales conversion rate studies show that 80% of all sales are done on the 5th to 8th reach. When I learned this statistic, my business completely changed! I learned that if I wanted to succeed, I needed to expect 5-8 conversations before doing so. And guess what? I used Facebook Messenger to help me start those conversations. It also became my "little tracking device." Because our messages were chronological, I could easily keep track of my status when paired with my list of prospects.

Failure to follow up is the backdoor that everyone slips through in sales. When prospecting online, it can be difficult to remember the state of every outreach. As a result, we often forget to follow up. Enter – The Penny App. This app helps close the door. It is similar to a virtual assistant in that it reminds me of who I need to follow up with when . . . a complete game changer!

When I follow up, the conversation becomes the "Polite Reminder" that I was there if they "needed" me. I experienced success by being very real and straightforward with my prospects. People don't mind an agenda; they do mind a hidden one! I encourage you to be straightforward and honest and remember to make the discussion about them and how you can add value to their life. Here's the big secret—NEVER end with "let me know!" That's the kiss of death in this business. Ask a question! Ask to follow up! You may get a "No," but that's one step closer to a YES! An objection is an opportunity to have a discussion, so welcome it!

3. Developing Trust. This opportunity involves putting yourself out there and getting comfortable with being a little uncomfortable. In my business, trust is a HUGE factor. So how do you build that electronically? How do you build that with people you don't really know that well? You do it by being yourself. Speak to your network as if you would be speaking to them at a dinner party. Find out what makes you tick and what you stand for, and then share about it!

I have always made it a priority to share with my network that I am about a lot of things, not just my business. I have allowed them into my life by sharing my cares and worries, achievements and failures, and I have always tried to add value to their day in some way. This is what fuels me. By sharing commonalities, as well as posting genuine things from the heart, I feel I have been able to develop positive, closer relationships. Have I been fearful at times to share too much? Sure! But I always bring it back to my faith and belief that we are in it together, so we should stick together. I believe this has allowed my network to know me and have the ability to trust me, which in turn has been an important aspect of my success.

When looking back at my career in Social Commerce, I have loved the journey of learning these things and developing rewarding relationships. Through peaks and valleys, I focused on what I could learn and how I could implement that into helping more people on my team succeed. This is a powerful business and a powerful platform that is continuing to change lives everywhere! I am rooting for each of you, and I applaud your stride in personal development by reading this book! I hope you are finding yourselves and your inner genius, because we are all born with one. Once you find your inner genius, the opportunities are endless!

MOMENTUM MAKERS

1. **BUILD YOUR BUSINESS THE WAY YOU WANT TO.** Soak up advice from those who have experienced success in running network marketing businesses. Read books on the network marketing model and industry, and study social media trends.

2. **GET CONNECTED ON SOCIAL MEDIA.** Use social media to make new connections and discover ways to help your network meet a need and add value to their lives.

3. **CREATE A POSITIVE TEAM CULTURE WITH YOUR TEAM.** Always put your teammates' goals ahead of yours. Encourage team camaraderie and do everything in your power to assist team members as they learn the process – this builds momentum and increases engagement.

4. **UTILIZE YOUR NETWORK.** Use social media platforms to connect with new and old friends. If you want to succeed, you need to expect 5-8 conversations before doing so. So, connect with others and add value to their life—it's everything!

5. **DEVELOP TRUST WITH YOUR NETWORK.** Trust is a HUGE factor, so allow your prospects into your life by sharing your cares and worries, achievements and failures. Try to always add value to their day in some way.

LAURA CAROFFINO
TAKING A CHANCE & BEING ALL IN

What if I told you I use to work in the Pentagon? Yes, the odd-shaped building full of government secrets, and that I worked with some of the most powerful people in our federal government at one time . . . and then one day I chose to give it all up to be a stay at home mom. You'd probably think I was crazy, which let's be honest we all are a little. Yes, it's true, I did, and I gave it all up so I could stay home with my children. When I left my dream job at the Pentagon, it was at that time that I had begun my research to look for jobs that I could work from home around my family's schedule. I had no clue at the time where this journey to work from home would take me, but it has led me on an amazing path to fulfillment, self-discovery, purpose, and of course, blessed me with financial freedom! Within this next chapter, I'm going to share some of my tips on how I've built a wildly successful business from home mainly through social media utilizing the power of network marketing.

From the time I was three years old I knew I was meant for something amazing. I originally thought it was a career within the federal government or perhaps even politics. Yes, I'm that crazy person that wanted to work within politics. To be honest, I actually dreamt of wanting to be the first woman President of the United States. I get some good reactions from people when I share that; I can only imagine what yours is too! Who knows, maybe I will still get that opportunity in the future, but my current path is one that I couldn't even fathom but I am so incredibly blessed that I was led in this direction. I think I owe my ambition to my parents, for it was their constant reminder that I can do anything I put my mind to. I am so thankful they always told me to set my goals high for I can do anything I set my mind to. For these reasons, I pushed myself and strived to be better, I just knew I was meant to help people in some capacity; I just never knew that the path I'd be on would lead me where I am today. Have you ever had that feeling that you knew you were destined for something amazing?

I thought I had my career plan perfectly mapped out and that nothing would move me away from the path that I had set for myself. However, after working years within the federal government, specifically the Department of Defense, I ended up leaving that career for my spouse's. My husband is in the military, and when we receive orders to move, unfortunately, like many military spouses, sometimes our careers just do not transfer to the next duty station, as was the case with mine. Having to constantly reinvent ourselves with each permanent change of station move, it begins to wear on oneself. With each move, I definitely started to lose my self-worth or purpose, one could say. This is something that many military spouses struggle with from the conversations I've had. It wasn't until I found network marketing that it all changed. Network marketing is the one industry that has enabled me to not only work from anywhere but it helped me find me again and provided me with an amazing purpose to help others.

I married my handsome Marine in 2004 and I'm a mom to five. I have four boys ages 18, 13, 3, and 3 months, plus one amazing daughter who is 16 years old. I have been home with them since 2007, shuttling them to school, activities, volunteering at their schools, and being there daily for them since leaving my career. On top of all that, I somehow manage to fit in my work around all of my family's daily activities including managing my multiple autoimmune disorders and hospitalizations. Yes, I have several rare autoimmune diseases, some of which are eventually fatal. Despite those constraints, I am able to work my business. Being able to work my business around my family's schedule is something I couldn't have done if I remained in my career. Finding network marketing has certainly been life changing but for the better. Having worked with high-profile military and political leaders my entire career up until 2007, I always thought that I would retire within the federal government . . . of course life had other plans for me, and for that, I am so very thankful.

I kind of found network marketing by accident. I was sitting in a hair salon getting my oldest's hair cut when I picked up a jewelry catalog. As I was flipping through it, I fell in love with all of the pieces within it. I turned the catalog over and read it was an opportunity to work from home. That piqued my curiosity because I had been commuting two hours one way to the Pentagon daily for years at this time and soon would have to leave my career due to us relocating across the country. I needed something that was transferable that I could do from home no matter where we may move. That day was the day that I was introduced to network marketing, I had no idea how that little catalog sitting at a beauty salon would change my life. I immediately joined that company as soon as I got home without even speaking to the consultant. When the consultant called me, she was shocked that by her leaving her catalog in public spaces actually worked! Yes, old school marketing still works today too. However, that company I was with in 2007 is not the same company I am with today. I may have went through one or two companies before I figured out how to properly market my business.

Back then I had no clue what I was doing and at the time social media was just becoming popular (hello MySpace and Yahoo groups). I thought social media was just for funny memes, and keeping in touch with old friends and family members back then, and I had no clue how powerful social media really could be. Honestly, I was one that fought hard against the idea of social media; it seemed very confusing at first. Plus, I wasn't very comfortable with putting my information out there in an unknown environment. Having worked within the intelligence community, the one thing that was engrained into me was to never put too much info out there, so sharing my story publicly on social media has been a challenge for me. Once I actually sat down and started to play with social media and really learn how it worked, I realized this actually could be the tool I needed to really make this working from home thing work. I just needed to figure out how to properly use social media for my business plus get over the fear of being seen online. Learning how to properly use social media in the beginning was something that was not for the faint of heart. It was painful for me, so if I can figure it out, you most definitely can too! It took me a few years of learning, research and growing to find the true way to market on social media. I, like many who start off at first, do it all wrong, oh so very wrong. I admit, I may have spammed one or two hundred people at first, and a few friends may have unsubscribed from my newsletters. Believe me, I felt that first unsubscribe, and it was a hurdle to get over at first. However embarrassing it may be looking back at the mistakes I made, they only taught me the correct way to utilize social media and how truly powerful it can be when done right.

Facebook is my go-to social media vehicle of choice and is what saved my business. Learning to market myself instead of a company or product is what made a huge change for me. It did take me years to really understand that concept though. Being able to leverage social media working from the convenience of a cell phone can literally change your life. In 2018, I was hit with a debilitating illness, one that would leave me with the inability to even walk at times. If it wasn't for the ease of network marketing and being able to work from my cell phone through social media, my business wouldn't be what it is today. I ended up being hospitalized in a foreign country for almost two full months, and all I needed was Wi-Fi and my cell phone and I was in business. Those two months hospitalized in a foreign country were two of my most successful business months, including even a huge rank promotion. You can really do anything if you have Wi-Fi, a cell phone, and very specific goals.

Social media has changed a lot over the years and what it is today will be very different in the future; it's a very fluid vehicle to use and being able to grow and adapt to the changes is key. If you can learn how to use one social media tool effectively and stay up to date with the constant changes, you will be very successful in marketing your business through social media.

My tips for utilizing social media and what is pivotal in my success is that I brand myself. I am selling myself and not my company or product. I utilize the 80/20 rule, which consists of 80% life and fun, because let's be honest, people are not using social media to buy stuff, they use it to socialize. Then while you're posting all the fun and life posts, sprinkle in about 20% of the time some information about your company and/or product without mentioning their names. Another great thing to share about is your team culture within network marketing—some join the industry to just meet new people, and posting about this could attract those looking for that friendship environment directly into your network marketing company. I know you're thinking, but how will they know what I'm selling or what company I'm with? Don't worry, curiosity will have them reaching out to you if you're doing it right, and that's our goal! You want your customers reaching out to you, not you chasing them. Imagine having a daily inbox full of people wanting to connect with you to buy and/or join your company? That's what is possible if you use attraction marketing properly.

Now not only has branding myself along with curiosity helped me grow a nine-figure organization within 2.8 years, but also being very on purpose and consistent. Consistency is the key to being successful in anything that you do. Have you ever tried to get into shape? It only worked if you ate healthy and exercised consistently, right? You wouldn't get in your ideal shape after 24 hours or even a week or two. It took consistent daily actions to get your desired results. This is the same concept; you must be consistent in your business by working your business daily in order to see success. Making your focus on income producing activities every single day. Also, be consistent with personal development for it will help you keep your mindset right, especially if you get a few "no's" here and there while you're learning. Most importantly, always be open to learning new strategies to work your business, especially on social media. Having a plan and purpose when on social media is key. Start rethinking how you utilize social media for it is a tool to market your business; be sure to not get stuck in a time suck scrolling. Set a time limit and be on purpose. Remember this is a tool you're using to make money online not waste your valuable time.

There are several components to being successful in network marketing utilizing social media, which are to always be actively prospecting new customers and teammates while utilizing attraction marketing, and most importantly being consistent. So many people say they have no one to talk to, but if you just expand your network through social media you can reach thousands. The main component to being successful online is being social through active prospecting using social media. Most people have a fear of meeting strangers on social media, but it's just like meeting someone in person. Just be yourself and connect with others. Start making meaningful comments on their posts to get to know them which in turn is building that relationship. I've actually met some of my closest friends on social media, either through groups, mutual friends or through the network marketing industry. Social media is an amazing tool to connect you with new people, if you use it properly.

Once you start actively prospecting you will meet so many new people on social media. Being purposeful while on social media through actively prospecting is exactly how I am consistently bringing in new people into my organization. One of the things that I could do while I was hospitalized in 2019 in Costa Rica, was meet new people online. My company is currently only in the United States so networking with people out of the country really wasn't helping my business just yet, but I am open to that still for future planning purposes of course. I would join groups on Facebook that interest me in some capacity. Once joining these groups, I become purposeful and active within that community. Building friendships through comments on posts and getting to know others within that group community is one of my top ways to build a very successful network marketing business plus make some incredible friends.

A few tips to keep in mind when you are prospecting on social media: the goal should be to get to know someone first not message them your link right away. That is a sure fire way to get put into Facebook jail and to be considered spam. Building a relationship will take time but once you develop the relationship you will know if they want more information about your product/offer or even joining you within your company. Most importantly, remember don't be a "spammy Pammy"; focus on connections and you'll do well on social media!

The second component to being successful with network marketing on social media is utilizing attraction marketing. Attraction marketing is having the ability to attract others to you through the stories that you share. Most people online utilize social media to post everything and anything. I highly recommend against that, and that you stick to positive content, or stories that have purpose to inspire others. People are attracted to positivity and positivity will give you positive results. For example, do you have that one friend, oh I'm sure you do, we all do, you know the one I'm talking about, the one that posts every complaint they have on social media? Do you avoid their feed? I know I do! Why is that? It is because negative posts create negative results. I know when I read a negative post it just puts me in a negative mindset, and I'd rather be upbeat, happy, and focused on what is possible. If you keep your posts to positive content you will have more people following you and not avoiding you. Remember people will buy from those they like, know, and trust so sharing your stories in a positive light will attract them to you.

Attraction marketing is a very easy concept once you get it down. It's just being authentically you and sharing your story or stories you believe your target market will respond well to. For example, in my case, I'm a military spouse that had to sacrifice her career for her spouse's. I utilize that story in a lot of my content online. I also utilize my illness to bring awareness and encourage others going through similar circumstances that you can be successful while going through some really rough health issues and that there is hope. Finding your voice and what you want to talk about is easy. Just take a moment and brainstorm your thoughts when you're sitting down planning your social media content. Here are a few ideas:

- Cooking

- What you read recently

- Beauty

- How to . . .

- Children

To figure out who you're trying to attract to you, also consider these ideas when writing your social media content:

- Who do you want to work with?

- What do they like?

- Do they have children?

- What problems do they have?

Those are just a few ideas to help you get started in planning your social media content to market your network marketing business. Just start jotting down a few ideas that you like to talk about, but remember to be positive and avoid overly political and religious topics as those could limit your customer base. Once you have your topics, then start doing some research so you can create some amazing positive social media content. Always remember that your personal social media profile is an extension of your business and you always want to put your best face forward. If you can spin it in a positive light to give people hope with whatever hardships you may be going through then share, your story may help someone who needs to hear it.

The third component to being successful in network marketing with social media is consistency. Consistency is where I see a lot of entrepreneurs struggle with social media. I admit, I've not always been consistent either, and when I'm not, my business suffers. I get it, life happens, and the solution to when things get busy is having a plan in place. Planning is a huge factor in being consistent and it also makes things a lot less stressful. Believe me, I have failed to plan before, and it is a struggle to get back into a rhythm. But if you make time to plan your social media content then it will be much easier for you to be consistent. Here are a few of my social media hacks for being consistent:

1. **Plan** - Take one day (usually the second to last Sunday of the month for me) to plan the next month in advance. This one task here saves me so much time and headache.

    a. Plan all social media posts, include lives as well (some platforms offer LIVE and highly recommend you schedule those as well) - topics are ok, we can do research later.

    b. Plan for 2 posts minimum daily. This keeps algorithms up.

    c. Schedule follow-up days for customers and prospects.

    d. Schedule reach out new connections (I do 10 daily).

    e. Schedule everything on your calendar including personal development.

2. **Utilize a social media posting platform** - this helps organize and plan your business posts on social media plus saves you a ton of time. A few scheduling programs that I like are Post My Party,

Trello, Cinchshare, and planoly. I use Cinchshare the most for both personal, business, and even group posts for groups that I personally manage, for example, my team pages.

These two things made a huge difference in my business and presence on social media, plus it gave me my time back. I am now very purposeful on social media and limit my time. My time is a valuable commodity and if I plan everything I do on social media out it saves me a lot of stress and time. Do you think you would be more effective in your business if you were less stressed?

If you are actively prospecting, utilizing attraction marketing and being consistent you will most certainly be successful with network marketing on social media platforms. If you're thinking you can't do this, believe me, you can, you just need to believe in this industry and most importantly believe in yourself. If you choose to take the time to learn and grow, you will be successful within this industry. Time is a big factor in this industry as well, for it may take you years to achieve success, and for most it does, for it won't happen overnight. The success stories you read about didn't happen overnight, there are years of learning and some struggling too that you're not seeing. Don't compare your chapter 1 to someone's chapter 20. What if you could earn a six- or seven-figure income? Would you be willing to give it your all for years at a time? Even if you don't have success right away? Keep in mind that those years will pass anyways so why don't you put 100% of yourself into this and jump all in? Imagine what your life would look like in five to ten years with a seven-figure income. What would that type of income do for you and your family? Is it worth the time and consistent effort to achieve? If you take the time and invest in yourself in learning how to market yourself online, you can create an amazing life for yourself and help others do the same. The opportunity is there and the choice is yours. Are you ready?

MOMENTUM MAKERS

1. **GOALS ARE IMPORTANT.** Having clear obtainable goals is key to being successful in this industry and in life. Write them down and put them where you can see them daily. This will help you reach each goal you set for yourself. Make sure your goals are measurable and realistic as well. Setting a small goal that builds to the next larger goal will help you achieve your goals faster.

2. **BELIEVE IN YOURSELF.** No matter what you do, believe in your ability to learn how to do something. You can do anything you put your mind to if you believe in yourself. One key way to help with your belief in oneself is to consistently do some type of personal development. Keeping your mindset right will be a key factor in your success.

3. **CONSISTENCY.** This one word I know has been said thousands of times, but it is true, if you are consistent with anything you can be successful. Make the effort to always touch some component of your business daily so that you form habits.

4. **TIME.** Time is a valuable commodity. Use your time wisely and work smarter not harder.

5. **BE AUTHENTICALLY YOU.** While you're present online and branding yourself, be you and true to you in everything you post or comment. Be authentically you. While you're present online and branding yourself, be you and true to you in everything you post or comment.

JESSICA HEFLEY

NOT LETTING YOUR PAST DETERMINE YOUR FUTURE

Where can an introvert make more than a brain surgeon, from their iPhone, in their yoga pants?

Talk about a headliner! Now, you may not have a testimony like that (YET), but grabbing your audience's attention is everything in a noisy world. This was actually the first line of a speech I gave on stage at our company's Convention speaking on behalf of the all those who had achieved the highest rank. I went on to ask the following questions and to see the show of hands in answer:

Were any of you not the popular one growing up? Never asked to prom? Didn't sit at the cool kid table at lunch? Picked last for sports teams growing up?

The power of connection, the power to be vulnerable and have your target audience say "me too" is one of the biggest ways to increase trust with your audience, especially over social media. You're not selling a product as much as you are selling a solution to their problem, maybe even a problem they didn't know they had. For me, I'm selling self-worth. I believe the real reason people aren't successful in life, in general and especially in network marketing, is because they don't believe in themselves. And they probably never really ever have, which is exactly why I strive to communicate that you CAN re-write your story. No matter what type of person you were or what circumstances you went through in your past, that does NOT have to be your future!

Network marketing was never on my radar because I thought of myself as an unlikely candidate for success. However, that was partly because I was still living out the story of "16-year-old Jessica" who wasn't popular, was shy, was never picked first, and was often in the shadows instead of the spotlight. But now I know for that very reason, I can relate and engage with more people because of the story of my past.

ENGAGE

Engage people in your story. Engage them in their stories. Engage in story. Story has a way to engage emotions more than facts ever could. What if the best social media strategy was YOU? As Brené Brown says, "Who you are is how you lead." This is where I believe most people miss the mark. It doesn't necessarily matter how many times a day you post or how long your LIVE videos are or what filter you use for your Instagram photos; if you're not evolving and growing, you will not be successful. People join YOU when they join a network marketing company. They join you because they see something in YOU that they want. Something in YOU adds value to their lives. My best social media strategy is to add value in everything you do. Be vulnerable enough to try new things, to fail, to learn, to grow, to evolve, to teach your audience something new, and to be relatable.

ENDURE

When I first started my network marketing business, I just knew that my husband would be supportive because of the income potential; I also knew that my five closest friends would do this with me, no doubt! After all, a couple of them desperately needed extra income: two of them had some pretty serious health issues I knew my supplements could help with, and one was working long hours in corporate America and found herself unexpectedly pregnant again with their second child just months after her first. Surely ALL of them would jump at this work-from-home opportunity to help others. It was a no-brainer in my book because they loved me, trusted me, and needed what I had to offer. Except all of them told me "no." I had to hear them say things like, "She's drunk the kool-aid," "this is going to be hard to watch," "she's embarrassing herself," "this is never going to work," and "I have to hit unfollow. It's just too painful to watch."

And this is what separates the amateurs from the professionals: endurance. Day after day, month after month, I kept posting on social media. Day after day, month after month, I kept watching training videos and reading books on network marketing, sales, and leadership. I endured when it was the hardest, when those closest to me didn't believe in me or what I choose to do for a living. And because I endured, four of those five friends eventually came around and are top-ranking leaders on my team because I endured.

EMPOWER

People long for positivity in a world of such darkness. Inspire them to greatness; encourage them to believe in themselves. Remind them of THEIR greatness. Everyone wants to be around someone who makes them feel good about themselves. Did you also know confidence is a form of empowerment? Confidence is contagious. People feel safe around confident people because there is no guesswork. They know exactly what they are going to get. Empowering raises them up and inspires them to all that is possible, and the possibilities are limitless in network marketing.

EDUCATE

When someone teaches someone something new or something they didn't already know, they instantly gain SO much credibility in their eyes. Remember, you don't have to be miles in front of everyone or be an expert to teach someone something. You just have to be one step ahead of them in any area, just one step ahead. People tend to forget when they start network marketing that they also have a life outside of network marketing. Do you garden, cook, craft, collect, read, travel, or research? Teach your audience something they may not know about what interests you. And remember when something interests you, you tend to believe everyone else already knows what you know. False! Invite them in. Educate them and watch your credibility soar.

ENTERTAIN

If I laugh at the same thing someone else laughs at, we are instantly friends, or we at least have a connection, instant connection. I immediately have something in common with them, and their likability factor in my book goes way up. Don't take life too seriously. One of the quickest ways to increase engagement on social media is to put content up that people INSTANTLY comment on and share. Who doesn't like to laugh? Who doesn't love a good smile after a hard day? The world needs a little more fun, a little more laughter, a little more lightness, and a lot less of taking ourselves too seriously.

I will keep going to someone's social media channel over and over and over if they are engaging, if I've seen them endure, and if I feel empowered, educated, and entertained by them.

But my favorite topic of all is helping business professionals who are in a lull. Are you feeling stalled, stuck, or simply unmotivated? Are you on the brink of burn out or, if you're being completely honest, way past it? I was there, struggling with doubt, debt, and disconnection. I see you. I was you. You CAN get unstuck. You CAN live your ideal life and have an abundance of time, money, and connection. You may not know your worth yet, but you will! With the help of Jesus and a life coach, I spun my life, marriage, and career around. If I'm being honest, my life lacked peace, and without it my social media presence was flat and fake and forced. Network marketing has a way of revealing quite a few insecurities doesn't it?

I'm so thankful God revealed His true purpose for me by increasing my influence through network marketing and stretching me in every way imaginable. I now know I'm here on this earth as a success mindset coach to help other entrepreneurs find THEIR area of expertise, to help them uncover a life of calling, heal unhealthy money relationship issues, and walk in infinite possibilities for growth and impact. Look at it this way: imagine trying to drive a Ferrari with the emergency brake on. You'll continue to have a lot of tension, do some damage, and feel a lot of resistance until you really get to the root of the areas in your life and business (because they are connected) you have been avoiding, resisting, or running from. Let's not avoid those anymore; let's get your subconscious foot off your break and get to the root issues, with compassion, so you can fly ahead with less resistance. I'm forever grateful to network marketing for giving me my start. It is so fulfilling now to personally help guide and coach such phenomenal humans and entrepreneurs to success, starting with their mindset to make the ultimate impact on this world.

MOMENTUM MAKERS

1. **ENGAGE.** Are you engaging your audience in YOUR story, and are YOU growing as a person first and foremost? Add value in everything you do. Be vulnerable enough to try new things, to fail, to learn, to grow, to evolve, to teach your audience something new, and to be relatable.

2. **ENDURE.** Are you going to quit when those closest to you first tell you no? Endure and keep believing in yourself when it was the hardest, even when those closest to you don't believe in you or what you choose to do for a living.

3. **EMPOWER.** Are people becoming more confident in themselves because of your presence on social media? Inspire others to greatness; encourage them to believe in themselves. Remind them of THEIR greatness.

4. **EDUCATE.** Are you bravely acknowledging and sharing the value you have to add to the world to serve and help others? When you teach someone something new or something they didn't already know, you instantly gain SO much credibility in their eyes.

5. **ENTERTAIN.** When is the last time you shared a laugh with your audience? No seriously 😄, are you taking life too seriously? The world needs a little more fun, a little more laughter, a little more lightness, and a lot less of taking ourselves too seriously.

ANDREW EATON

EVEN IN THE DIGITAL WORLD, PEOPLE ARE STILL PEOPLE

My entire world started to change on September 22, 2008. My wife, Paula, and I were in the car on our way to spend a weekend in Swaziland to celebrate our first wedding anniversary. Just after going through the border into Swaziland, my phone rang. It was my business partner, who had just stepped out of a meeting with our funders. He informed me that they had pulled out of our business effective immediately, leaving us with no prospect of any payment at month's end. My heart stopped. That was the weekend I found out what being broke felt like.

On **the night** of September 23, 2008, the night of our anniversary, Paula and I shared a cocktail at the bar. That's correct. We shared a cocktail, not a dinner, because a cocktail was all we could afford. Can you imagine what that felt like?

Over the next few years, I worked for a company selling outdoor media while Paula worked her full time job as an HR manager for a listed company. Our combined salaries were barely enough to keep a roof over our heads. During this time, our two amazing children were born. Jenna was born in January 2009, and Angus arrived in July 2010. I found myself completely frustrated financially, but I had fallen into a comfort zone. I guess you could say I had become COMFORTABLY UNCOMFORTABLE.

In 2011 our world was turned upside down when Paula and I were told that our little girl, Jenna, was autistic. Everything changed!

I realized that if we were to give Jenna everything she deserved in her life to overcome her challenges, I would have to make some significant changes. It was going to take a lot of money and time, neither of which we had. I had no money to invest anywhere and was fresh out of any good business ideas.

Having dabbled a little in Network Marketing in the past, I decided to investigate it more thoroughly. I started doing research and discovered a company I felt I could partner with. To me it was a no brainer. Our problems were solved! Now I just had to break the news to Paula. Naturally, she was completely horrified, as she simply didn't believe in Network Marketing. Apparently neither did my father in law, who decided to invite me for a round of golf during which he promptly attempted to talk me out of Network Marketing all together. Looking back, I can completely understand why he and Paula were so concerned. I hadn't exactly been a massive success story up to that point, and most people only hear stories about how many people fail at Network Marketing. Very rarely do they hear the success stories. However, I knew that I would not become a statistic; the only way this would fail was if I failed it. The burning desire to succeed, provide for my family, and give my children the lives that they deserved meant that NOTHING was going to stop me. My "WHY" was HUGE!

I had a clear vision driving my life. In my mind, if a doctor called from the Swiss Alps saying he had a cure for autism, but, to get it we'd have to take a 6-month trip and drink water from a specific stream in the Alps at a cost of $100,000, I would drop everything and do anything in my power to make it happen. This vision drove me every day!

And so my journey started. Kicking off part time, I started my Network Marketing career with absolute determination. You know the usual drive: making a list of two hundred people, calling it, making another list, this time your chicken list (all those you were afraid to contact on the first list), and then calling them. My days consisted of waking up, scarfing down breakfast, rushing to work, coming home in the evening, making my calls, and going to meetings—every day, every week, every month. I had no life, but I had a big WHY. As most network marketers know, I received a lot more "no's" than "yes's" but just enough "yes's" to keep me motivated to keep going. Within eight months, I was making more money from my part-time business than I was in my full-time job. It was time to quit, and in May 2012 I handed in my resignation.

Then came my next challenge. My warm market had started to dry up, and I found myself wondering how I was going to find more leads. I realized that social media was the answer. To me, Facebook and Linkedin were a virtual representation of a huge networking function, and the more connections I made and conversations I started, the more opportunities I would create to talk to people about my business. After all, all business is just conversation. My strategy was very simple. I first connected, then I started a conversation, and at the appropriate time, I spoke to them about my business. Keep in mind, I engaged in many conversations. I asked people many questions about themselves. I showed an interest in them, and only after getting to know them would I bring my business into the conversation. I NEVER spammed people. Too many people make the mistake of "throwing up" on people on social media.

In 2013, I purchased a course by my now good friend and mentor, Todd Falcone, called "How to Recruit Professionals." It was a course that would change my business and my life. One line in the entire course was instrumental in helping me recruit over 300 people on Facebook and Linkedin within 12 months. At the appropriate time in the conversation, I would simply say, "Hey Bob, I realize that this is a complete shot in the dark, and I am not even sure this is a fit, but may I ask you if you at all keep your options open in terms of other ways of making money?" This was the perfect line I needed to transition from a casual Facebook or Linkedin conversation to a business conversation. I hardly found any people who were not open, and it worked like a BOMB!

I soon realized that recruiting was just one skill I needed in order to grow a Network Marketing business, and I quickly started to burn out because nothing I was doing was duplicating my success in any way. As much as I was recruiting, very few people in my team were doing the same, and loads more quit after a month or two. I needed a solution and had no upline to turn to, as my sponsor and his upline had quit the business within a month of sponsoring me.

One of the best things I ever did was to always take 5 percent of my earnings and invest it in personal and skills development. In 2015, this is what led me to meeting Masa Cemazar and Miguel Montero, who soon became big mentors of mine. They took one look at my business and said the reason I was not duplicating was because I needed a system. At that stage, I was earning between $3000 and $4000 per month, and over the next twelve months Masa and Miguel helped me build my system. By 2016, I had managed to create duplication and became a 6-figure income earner.

However, 2016 also came with more difficult news. Our son, Angus, was also diagnosed with autism. The reality of having two autistic children really hit me, and this drove me even harder.

Network Marketing is, simply put, the best personal development course in the world, cleverly disguised as a business opportunity. I whole heartedly embraced personal and skills development to a much higher level, and it was through this journey that I was fortunate enough to find Eric and Marina Worre from Network Marketing Pro. I will forever be grateful to them as they helped me take my thinking and my business to the next level—a level I would never have imagined only a few years earlier. If I was only ever allowed to give one piece of advice, it would be to find mentors and change the way you think.

Over the years, I have never stopped using social media as my main platform and continue to use it in its simplest form:

1. Connect

2. Start a conversation

3. At the appropriate time, ask Todd's Question

4. Send a marketing link

5. Follow up

6. Put on a 3-way call with your closer or "money man"

MY DAILY ROUTINE

Let me elaborate.

Every day I strive to connect with a minimum of 20 new people on Facebook and LinkedIn. I don't do more as that can lead one to be thrown in Facebook or LinkedIn "jail". A connection is merely a friend request.

Every day I start a conversation with all the people who have responded to my Connect Request. Remember, it's a big banquet room, so I don't throw up on them. A simple, "Hi John, great to meet you. Thanks for accepting my friend request. How are you?" is more than enough! The art of the conversation lies in asking the right questions. Social Media guru, Frazer Brookes, uses the best acronym: LORD. I always start by asking people where they are LOCATED. Where are they from? What's it like living there? How long have they lived there for? Then I move on to OCCUPATION. What do they do for a living? Do they enjoy it? Any challenges? After that (and only if I feel they will be comfortable or if I feel I need to, as often the L and the O are enough) I move on to RECREATION. What do they do for fun? Does their job give them enough time to enjoy recreation? And lastly, if needed I speak about their DREAMS. What would they love to do if they had all the choices in the world? Where would they love to travel to if budget was not a criterion?

At any point during the LORD process I may get a feel as to it being the right time to ask Todd's question, and it is at this time that I am able to transition the chat into a business chat.

From there I send them the link to our information and agree a time for us to have a follow up discussion. I set a goal of sending out at least three links a day from my Facebook and LinkedIn conversations.

I follow up at the agreed time EXACTLY and ask them what they liked most about what they saw. Usually they will tell me and then have a few questions. (Again, I set a goal of a minimum of three follow ups a day out of the links I have sent out.)

And, lastly, here lies the most important part of the process. I DO NOT answer their questions. I simply edify an upline or downline leader to help me close them. I edify my "money man" and I get them on a 3-way Zoom call as soon as possible. I NEVER try and close my own prospects. This is vitally important because it shows the prospect that they will never have to close their own prospects either and makes them feel they can do it.

Engaging in this system and teaching it to my team has been instrumental in helping me create a 7-figure Network Marketing business. Our children now have a fulltime mom, who pours her life into giving them the best chance of curing their condition. Network Marketing has given us the time and money to enable her to do this, and as recently as 2019, we had our "Swiss Alps" moment where both Paula and I were able to take almost 2 months off over the course of the year and take our children to specialists in various parts of South Africa for weeks at a time. Time and money are not an issue or a challenge. I shudder to think where our children would be if I had not made that decision in 2011 and if Paula and I were still both working fulltime jobs. We have been able to move away from the demands of big city living to our dream home at the ocean, surrounded by a community who love our children and sow into their lives. My son, Angus, dreams of being a big wave surfer just like his idol, Chris Bertish, and despite his condition, we have been able to offer him the opportunity of fulfilling his dream. Our daughter, Jenna, loves fishing in the rock pools, which are now only 300 meters from our front door.

Network Marketing can change your life if you allow it to. You will have many dream stealers and many people who think you are crazy, but if you have a big enough WHY, their opinions won't matter. Strive to be a professional; invest in personal and skills development. Don't try to reinvent the wheel. Just follow the system.

Network Marketing isn't easy, but it is simple. You can do it!

———————— MOMENTUM MAKERS ————————

1. **TREAT PEOPLE LIKE PEOPLE!** Remember, just because the person you are speaking and connecting with is sitting behind a computer or phone screen half way across the world, they are still a person! They are NOT a virtual person. Treat them like a real person.

2. **VISUALIZE THE SOCIAL MEDIA PLATFORM YOU ARE ENGAGING IN AS ONE BIG BANQUET HALL.** I always visualize that I am in a big banquet room full of people. I know I need to "work" the room and chat to as many people as I can. I am only there to collect business cards and form relationships. Your goal is to CONNECT with people.

3. **DON'T VOMIT ON PEOPLE!** You wouldn't walk around a banquet hall vomiting your business opportunity on everyone you talk to would you? By the end of the evening you would have every person in that room running away from you when they see you approaching. So, why would you vomit your business opportunity on people you have just meet on a social media platform?

4. **BE INTERESTED IN THEM!** If you were "working" the banquet hall successfully, you would be engaging in conversation with people and asking them questions about THEM. Do the same in this "Virtual Banquet Room". Ask the LORD questions.

5. **BE CONSISTENT AND PERSISTENT!** Stay the course. 20 new connections a day. Don't stop after 1 week or even 1 month. Make it a daily habit. Don't even look up until a year has passed. Do this and you will never run out of people to talk to on social media.

CODI BILLS

SOCIAL GAME SUCCESS

I was just a small-town girl, living in a lonely world . . . Okay, not really, but I felt that way! Nearly a decade ago, I was on the verge of depression. I was a mother of 4 young boys, trapped in the house with a non-existent social life. I adored my husband and kids, but I felt like something was missing in my life, like there was something more I could be doing. I had so much to give, and I was tired of hiding my talents and feeling lost with zero confidence.

At the time, social media was just in its early phases. As I explored these platforms, they opened my eyes to the network marketing world. Facebook allowed me to instantly connect to new friends and reconnect with old friends. It was then that I started seeing women in various companies posting about their direct sales opportunities.

I was always a little bit skeptical and naive when it came to direct sales and MLM companies. I had no idea how they worked, and I thought it was just a bunch of hype. I also didn't realize how much effort, heart, and soul people put into these business opportunities in order to be successful.

Fast forward to when I made the decision to actually try one of these network marketing companies. I went into it blindly, and I didn't even tell my husband. I didn't even know anything about the compensation plan and the process, but I knew I would enjoy the social aspect of it. And I did! I had so much fun gathering with other women and sharing my product. My husband immediately saw a change in me, and people started recognizing me around town and saying, "Hey, you're THAT girl!"

This lit off a light bulb in my head as to how powerful my social media presence was, so I ran with it and took it to the next level. I used the name people associated me with and made it my personal brand on Facebook and Youtube. My sales went through the roof, and I built a team of powerhouse women. What started as a hobby to get out of the house turned into a full-blown career as I built an empire together with my team.

This soon provided me with an amazing income, recognition, trips, new friends, and confidence! I was a better wife and mother because I felt challenged and rewarded, something that I believe every woman needs! This gave me an avenue to set goals and to lead and inspire women just like me who needed something more in their lives. In fact, just within the last year, my personal motto manifested itself: "Dreams before dishes." The dishes can wait, but your dreams can't! It was always there in the back of my mind, but it wasn't until recently that I actually put it into practice. My personal motto has led me to be a 7-figure earner and an inspiration to other women who need a push to get past the little things that hold them back from achieving their hopes and dreams!

Network marketing, when done right, can open so many doors. I have soared to the top of each company that I have been with, and the #1 reason is because of the power of social media and the way I have marketed myself within it. When I look back at how I have achieved these things, I can identify 5 key things that got me there. I call them "Codi's 5 C's."

COUNTENANCE

Ask yourself how you hold yourself on your social media platforms. Do you take a negative stance on your posts? Are you portraying a fake personality? What you say online paints the expression of and becomes your virtual face. You could be the most beautiful person physically, but unless you're putting out meaningful messages on social media, your looks mean nothing.

It's hard to do, but reflecting positivity and reality in everything you post will carry you far in network marketing. And remember, once you put something online, it's out there forever! Also keep in mind that online interactions are the same as face-to-face interactions. Are you the same person online as you are in person? For example, no one wants to be served at a restaurant by a grouchy and inattentive waiter. And hanging out with someone who is negative all the time and is never happy is such a drag. Your network will dwindle if you are a negative or sad person all the time on social media.

It's also very hard, but really impactful, to remain neutral on political issues. You'll lose followers, teammates, and customers if your strong opinions differ from theirs. Most people think that they can sway others toward their point of view by posting on social media, but it actually discredits them and opens doors for confrontation and contention.

It's simple! Be upbeat, happy, and positive! But make sure it is real and genuine. People can sniff out when someone is being fake.

CONFIDENCE

People are attracted to confident people who have a clear message. Your word choices can make you appear confident, but on the other hand, they can make it look like you aren't so sure about what you are sharing. You wouldn't want to join someone's team who says things like "I think you'll succeed at this" or "you might succeed at this" or "maybe you will succeed at this" would you? It sounds so much better when you post "I know you will succeed at this" or "You will succeed at this" or "You'll definitely succeed at this."

You also need to make sure you are confident in how you talk about yourself! It's always good to build yourself up on social media, if done in a motivating and genuine way without coming across as rubbing your success in everyone's faces. Share a story, be relatable, and make sure what builds you up is also motivating to someone else. People need to know that what you do is something they can duplicate.

Confidence in your product is important, too. You show lack of confidence when you simply post websites, pictures, and prices. Sharing an impactful story about what you are offering makes a bigger impression, and people will be more confident in you and your message. They will trust you.

Whenever you feel a lack of confidence, just listen to what you are saying to yourself and others and make simple changes to your word choices if your message is not coming across as confident and positive. It will switch your mindset for the better!

Give yourself a pep talk every day! Your mindset is the first thing you need to work on when you wake up each morning. It will set the tone for how your day will go. When your head starts getting in the way of your heart, then it's time to put some positive affirmations back in your mind. It takes a lot of self-control to not post rants online. Facebook is often mistaken for a diary. Don't air out your dirty laundry on there!

CONNECTION

The way you connect with people on social media determines how successful you will be. The whole point of being on social media is to connect with others, so why not do it right?! You wouldn't walk up to a stranger and immediately start giving your business pitch, so why would you do that to a stranger online?

It's not going to help you to reach out to huge masses of people; rather, it's best to find people that you jive with, then begin to develop a relationship with them.

So what does this look like? It's staying engaged on their posts, personal messaging, and networking with them. Comment on their posts, ask questions about them, and find similar ground to build on.

Not everyone you make a connection with will join you, but if that relationship is strong, you'll have a business friend for life. You can never have enough support, and you can never support others enough. Referrals will come your way over and over again! The key to connecting is to think about others, not yourself. What is it that you can offer to better their lives?

CALIBER

Does your level of ability shine through on social media? Does it look like you know what you are doing? Staying educated and up-to-date on the ever-changing algorithms in each social platform is so important. This determines if your posts are being seen, and it determines if people will take you seriously.

Another aspect of caliber is what you look like, what your workspace looks like, and what your lifestyle looks like. Having a good profile picture goes a long way! Never judge a book by its cover does not apply here! Your profile is your first impression. Can people clearly see what you do, what you stand for, what your personality is like, and what your brand is just by looking at your profile?

When you go live, what does your background look like? You may not realize that your viewers are observing your surroundings. Good lighting, a clean area, and a space free from noise and distraction adds a professional touch to your message. For example, if I am watching a proclaimed leader in the industry go live about how they are living their best life and making a big income, but their background or environment doesn't align with that, I'm not going to take them seriously or believe what they are saying.

People are all about lifestyle, so take advantage of all of the resources out there that will filter your pictures and improve the technology that you use to get your business out there.

In a nutshell, stay educated on new social media developments and be professional in what you say and how you look.

CONSISTENCY

Harvey Mackey said, "If you are persistent you will get it. If you are consistent you will keep it."

Going days or even weeks without having a presence on social media will confuse your team, your customers, and your potential teammates. If this happens, it's really hard to play catch up! Putting together a schedule of posts can help with this. Always stay in front of it!

Being consistent in your message will help avoid confusion. Do you practice what you preach? Do you walk the walk and talk the talk daily? Is your brand consistent across all of your social platforms? It's important to maintain visual and emotional consistency in everything you post. Be sure to know your target audience and be consistent with those to whom you are speaking.

Being consistently engaged with your followers is of top importance! Replying and commenting on your post interactions and on those of your followers makes them feel relevant and gives you credibility. Set time aside to do this each day.

Before you post, ask yourself if what you are posting can add value to someone else and if it aligns with your message and brand.

Now that we've gone through the 5 C's of social media, what will you do with them? Applying what you learn is how changes are made. I don't believe anyone is an expert in anything because there is always something new to learn and ways to grow and develop. If you change nothing, nothing will change.

Create a plan and don't let anything stop you. Being a full-time mom has never stopped me! I have developed ways to incorporate and adapt my business into my family life without having to give up our time together. It's possible! Strategically use social media to your advantage and stop holding yourself back. Don't put your dreams on hold because they won't always be there.

Do you really want success, and how bad do you want it? Are you willing to put in the time? I know you do, otherwise you wouldn't be reading this book. So go conquer the world!

——— MOMENTUM MAKERS ———

1. **CONFIDENCE.** Consumers and potential teammates are attracted to one who is confident and has a clear message. If you are unsure of what you represent or sell, how can they be sure about you? Sharing an impactful story about what you are offering makes a big impression, and people will be more confident in you and your message. They will trust you.

2. **CALIBER.** Your character is determined by the level of your abilities, and they must shine through as you market yourself and your business. So, stay educated on new social media developments and be professional in what you say and how you look.

3. **COUNTENANCE.** Decide how you want to be known inside and outside of your business. How do you hold yourself on social media? Would people trust you enough to work with you? Do you walk the walk and talk the talk? Reflecting positivity and reality in everything you post will carry you far in network marketing.

4. **CONNECTION.** The way you connect with people will always determine your outcome or success. Do you want a block or a conversation? What kind of online relationships are you developing with people? It's best to find people that you jive with, then begin to develop a relationship with them.

5. **CONSISTENCY.** Show up everyday! Don't confuse your followers by not having a plan and sticking to it. Set aside time every day to be consistently engaged with your followers, which makes them feel relevant and gives you credibility.

JESSIE WELTE

SHARING IT ALL — THE GOOD, THE BAD & THE UGLY

When I was little and someone would ask me what I wanted to be when I grew up, I said an Astronaut. As I grew older, my love for *Ally McBeal* (who remembers that show?) dominated, and my desire to fight the good fight in the court room took over. I majored in English as a freshman in college with the hopes to attend law school. I was 17. Four years and four major changes later, I graduated at the ripe age of 21 with a degree in business, more specifically hospitality and tourism management. It was a long cry from defense attorney, but my classes were Wine Tasting and Culinary Arts, so who could blame me? If you would have told me that 16 years later I'd be a professional network marketer, I would have been very confused. I had never heard the term before. Network marketing was a foreign concept to me, but it is what saved my life. Oh Jessie, you are being SO dramatic. Saved your life? Yes, saved my life.

MY STORY

When I started my business almost 6 years ago, I was highly depressed. I was a small business owner helping my husband, Brody, run a stand up paddle boarding company. He started his business in 2009 after being laid off in the recession. We were living that entrepreneur life, following "our dreams" (insert his dreams), but it was hard. We struggled to make ends meet, putting most of our life on credit cards and prayers. Two cross country moves, a whole lot of stress, and two kids later, I learned that I wasn't a good risk taker. I had zero faith in the American dream, and I had the ability to make any situation seem bleak. I was a reallllly good version of myself in those days. I was a tightly bound ball of stress and anxiety. In the middle of building my husband's dream and raising kids on an extremely fixed budget with absolutely no safety net, I had around 48,038 panic attacks and even more sleepless nights. My life, in my eyes, was falling apart at the seams. I felt like I was treading in shark infested waters. Did I mention I can be dramatic?

When I was approached to join a network marketing company in 2014, the timing could not have been better. I was swimming in the water of my own tears, a struggling wife and mom. I was desperate for SOMETHING to save me. Raising kids, wanting more, being jealous of everyone else who seemed to have it all, I lived my days in a not so bright place. I was just a ticking time bomb full of potential, ready to explode if I didn't find something for myself. I was ready to re-write my story. Was I skeptical? Sure! I had done the whole small business thing before, and to be honest, I wasn't looking forward to building another business. But my unhappiness and dissatisfaction with my current situation were a much louder voice in my head than the one of doubt, so I signed up. I signed up because I could do this business from my home, alongside my kids. I signed up because deep down in my gut I knew that while this might not solve all my problems, it was a start. I was ready to make changes in my life, and this was the only opportunity sitting at my feet, so I grabbed it and I ran. I had zero marketing or sales experience and absolutely no knowledge of my company's product to rely on. I grew my business on grit and grace. I grew it because I HAD to; there was literally no other option for me.

In just 18 months I hit the very top of my company's pay plan. I was earning more than I could have ever imagined, feeling more confident in my skin than I have in my entire life, and I was making my dreams come true. I transitioned from treading water to sailing through it. Was it easy? No, of course not! Nothing good ever is. How did I do it? I became obsessed. I was obsessed with my business. I was driven, determined, and unapologetically in love with the person that I was becoming because of it. I committed 100%; I was all in. I studied my product. I picked up books about network marketing (like this one you're reading now). I became a student of the business. Social media was my platform.

You won't find one business today that doesn't have a social media account. I knew that it was a sure fire way to reach a lot of people. I knew NETWORKING was going to be my friend. I quickly started re-connecting with high school friends, my field hockey teammates, my honors English classmates . . . all of them. I racked my brain to remember the names of people I went to elementary school with, old neighbors, sorority sisters, co-workers, even ex-boyfriends made the cut. I grew my "social" network.

Some of the most amazing people on my team have come from my network's network, people who were introduced to me through someone else, complete strangers. Never forget your life can be changed by a complete stranger. Your life can be changed because you introduced your high school math teacher to your product and they became a lifelong customer. Your life can be changed because of a social media post that your childhood neighbor related to then asked a few questions and decided to join you. Your life can be changed because a friend shared your post and someone *she* went to college with sees it and becomes intrigued. Your job is to share, to invite, and to allow people from all different backgrounds to hear your story because your story just might look a lot like theirs. This was something I knew I could leverage on social media. I was struggling. I had debt. I was unhappy, unfulfilled, and unsatisfied. I knew others had to be too. I simply shared all the parts of my journey, in the hope I could connect with people.

I knew it was important to get people to follow me on social media. I knew that being real was the key. I had to allow people to see all the parts of my life, the good and the bad. Being relatable was SO important to me. I began crafting my brand. I needed to be entertaining so people would tune in. I had to be inspiring so people would come back. I posted about my life as a mom. I was vulnerable and shared the moments when I felt like I was failing. I talked about wanting more children but not being able to afford it. I talked about why I decided to try my company. I talked about applying for WIC when finances were particularly low (this was very uncomfortable). Funny enough, I found being open to be therapeutic. I also found a ton of support. I continued to share my life through social media, sprinkling in my product and company opportunity in the midst. I disclosed my favorite crockpot recipes and my fears as my second child started to show signs of Autism. I shared my excitement when my business was able to pay off my student loan. I discussed my elation when we were making enough money that having a 3rd child didn't seem so crazy anymore. All the while, people were watching. I had used social media as a sort of blog of my journey. They got to travel alongside me as I shared my past and current struggles, as well as my victories.

The beauty in sharing the not so colorful times in my life was that when things improved, when my life started to get better, people were there cheering me on. People were invested in my journey, seeing themselves in my story, curious about the one constant during all the change, my business. The seed was there, and now thanks to my branding, openness, and vulnerability on social media, it was beginning to grow. As my success grew, the belief bubble my network had for this type of industry grew. There are a lot of jaded people out there with stories on how direct sales failed them, but the truth is, the ONLY way you fail at a business like this is if you quit. Bottom line: you can be successful. You can grow a substantial income from home selling a product you believe in. You just can't give in to the naysayers. You can't waiver in your belief of what you are selling. You can't give up when you hear "no" thousands of times or get ignored over and over again. As long as you do something every day, are consistent and willing to work and learn this industry, constantly changing with times, and constantly growing as a person and business owner, you will have success.

Social media is a huge tool that we all have. If you use it correctly (see my tips below) and squeeze every ounce of potential out of it, it can be the catalyst to that success.

SOCIAL MEDIA TIPS

Be open. The key to my success was having people root for me. I let them know my darkest days so that they could appreciate the brightest with me. I wanted people to see me, my faults, my fears, and my failures. I needed them to become invested in my journey so that when I started to change, they noticed. They needed to see a direct correlation between my newfound positivity and my business. My life went from black and white to color, and my company held the paint brush. Do not be afraid to be vulnerable and to talk about the uncomfortable things. Something was missing in your life that you felt needed to be filled. Share that. The truth is someone will connect with you; someone will see themselves in your story, but only if you share it. You have a chance to reach out and touch people's lives. Once they feel that connection, the curiosity in your business will grow. They will want the same changes, and they will be open to hearing how you grew your business and what that could mean for them too.

Be relevant. Don't overthink your social media brand, but make sure it's meaningful. You want content that people want to tune in to. If you give entertaining, inspiring, educational, and (my favorite) REAL posts and stories, then people will find value in your content. People will tune in to your story. They will watch your stories and comment on your posts. They key is to hook them. Get them invested and entertained, so they trust you; you become a part of their day. When you post about your product or company, they are there; they are watching. You want people to fall in love with you so they fall in love with what you are selling.

Focus on what makes you unique. Your social media presence should be a window into your life; it should be about what you are passionate about. Your business is 100% one layer of you, but you can't focus only on that, or people won't stay tuned in. Maybe you love to run, or cook, or knit. Perhaps you are involved in your church or you are a mom or a fitness lover. What makes up your life? My advice is to take 5 things and develop your brand around those.

Keep working to expand your network and make new connections. Seek others who have your interests through hashtags. If you are a mom who loves to run, your posts should have certain hashtags to attract moms who love to run: #momrunner #momprenuer #momswhorun #naptimehustle #runningmom. Your most powerful business partners will be the people you find along the way who are like you. Why? Because they relate to your story. Start developing content for your social media posts and stories around the idea of attracting yourself.

Never stop learning. Social media is constantly evolving. When I started five years ago, the biggest tool we had was Facebook. Now, we've seen this huge shift toward Instagram not to mention Snapchat, Twitter, and TikTok, and I am sure in the next 5 years many other platforms will emerge. Your job is to stay on top of it. Be ready to learn a new app, a new way of running your business. The beauty of social media is that it's a free way to market and promote your product and business, and it is right at your fingertips. The curse is we all have it. You need to have that edge; you need to be able to keep up with the changing times and latest and greatest. Most people won't. Most people will not take the time to learn, and that's where you can get the upper hand. Remember, this is your business, and if you aren't constantly working to improve how you run it to reach a new audience, expand your network, and attract new partners and customers, then you are behind. I remember when Instagram stories first started getting out there and I thought, "Oh great, another thing I have to learn how to do." I fought it. I sort of refused to learn. Then it became apparent that they weren't going anywhere and I was behind. Now they are the main way I promote my product. They are what I watch now instead of TV at night. Don't get behind on new technology.

If you want this to truly work for you, it can. If you want a network marketing business to grow an income, a lifestyle, a legacy, then you can. Take a page from my book (or chapter) and become obsessed with evolving into the best version of yourself. Be ready to work, be vulnerable, be ready to talk to people, and always be ready to learn new things. Remember that the only way you fail is if you quit! Network marketing can be the vehicle to change your life, but never forget that you are the driver.

MOMENTUM MAKERS

1. **BE VULNERABLE IN SHARING YOUR STORY; IT WILL HELP OTHERS CONNECT TO YOU.** People will get to travel alongside you as you share your past and current struggles, as well as your victories. Your job is to share, to invite, and to allow people from all different backgrounds to hear your story because your story just might look a lot like theirs.

2. **BE YOURSELF AND BE REAL!** When you give entertaining, inspiring, educational, and (my favorite) REAL posts and stories, then people will find value in your content.

3. **KEEP MAKING NEW CONNECTIONS.** Never stop expanding your reach. Seek others who have your interests through social media hashtags. Your most powerful business partners will be the people you find along the way who are like you.

4. **ALWAYS IMPROVE YOUR CRAFT BY STUDYING THE BUSINESS.** This is your business, and if you aren't constantly working to improve how you run it to reach a new audience, expand your network, and attract new partners and customers, then you are behind.

5. **BECOME OBSESSED WITH YOUR BUSINESS AND THE PERSON IT'S SHAPING YOU TO BE.** Will it be easy? No, of course not! Nothing good ever is. But if you want this to truly work for you, it can!

MALLORY GARSHNICK

DON'T GET STUCK AT BASE CAMP

When I first started my network marketing business, I had NO experience as a business owner. No sales experience. No social media presence. I wasn't a blogger with a huge following or a small business owner who knew the ins and outs of owning a business. I was single, in my late-twenties, practicing full-time as a dentist, and living my dream in a condo in downtown Seattle. If you had stopped me on the streets of Pike Place Market and told me I'd be a top leader in a Network Marketing company within the next 5 years, I would've told you, you were crazy, and I would have kept on daydreaming about my dream house on top of the beautiful (and expensive!) Queen Anne Hill. So before network marketing, how was I going to get to this dream life? By being my own boss, of course, by owning my own practice. Up next on my checklist was searching for the perfect practice with a broker. Little did I know, that venture included practices with million-plus dollar price tags. On top of my soaring student loan debt? Yikes. The thing that scared me the most about all of it, though, was committing to living in Seattle for the remainder of my career.

I'm from Florida originally and went to undergrad and dental school in Florida. Almost all of my family lives there, and it's all I had ever known. But that little voice deep inside of me told me to get out there and explore. I like to call these inner urgings "God whispers." You know, the nudges and soft pushes you feel telling you to go in one direction or another, toward a new experience, or maybe away from something or someone risky. I heard them calling me to the west coast, and although it seemed scary, since I'd never lived more than 45 minutes from my hometown, I listened. Searching for adventure and something new and different, I picked up and moved diagonally across the country after graduation with $5000 in my pocket (I was RICH!) . . . and no job.

Like any transition, it took a little while to acclimate. I bought a jacket on my very first day in town (why would anyone need a jacket in JUNE?!), but apparently summer doesn't start in Seattle until July 5th. I learned so much during those 2 years, and while I loved the Pacific Northwest, the thought of never returning to the Sunshine State was concerning. Owning my own practice was placed on the backburner for the time being since the price tags and commitments were too large, and I kept working for other people. You might imagine that as someone with an entrepreneurial spirit, working for others wasn't exactly a dream come true for me. While I'm so very thankful for the jobs and experiences I had, I couldn't extinguish that burning desire from deep within to be in charge and to do it my way (another "God whisper").

A few months later, an old friend called out of the blue to tell me more about her business, which was expanding out West. I can still remember the exact bench I was sitting on during my lunch break at work when she explained the ins and outs of her new journey. I was intrigued. "Well, do you know anyone who might be a good fit for this?" she asked. "Um, what about me?!" I said. Within a week I had purchased a business kit and launched my new venture. It was my first experience in Network Marketing. I didn't have a clue what I was doing, but I knew I didn't have to give up dentistry to start it. More importantly, I didn't have to shell out a million dollars; I didn't have to commit to living in one place for 40 more years, and I didn't have to hire employees, build a website, or ship products. It was a business in a box! The only thing I knew I had to do was be coachable, to be open to learning about this industry, this company, and these products.

My friend was soaring her way to the top of our company, and I knew I wanted to follow in her footsteps. "Show me what you did, and I'll do it," I promised, and I couldn't have been more sincere. Every day she'd give me a checklist, and every evening I'd call and ask "what's next?" I remember the first time she asked me to help lead a training call for our team. I use the term "lead" very loosely. I wasn't doing much of anything. It was a mock 3-way call. All I was supposed to do was play the role of the prospect on the training call. She had given me two questions ("objections," really) to ask, and that was my entire speaking role. You would've thought I had been chosen to star on *Naked and Afraid* and was just dropped off in the jungles of South America. I was sweating bullets and pacing around my 700 sq. ft. studio apartment as I shakily mumbled something like, "I don't know, Sally. I'm really busy. What if I don't have time for adding something else to my plate?" After the call was over and the sweating had ceased, I realized I had survived. It might sound silly to you that this was such a big deal to me at the time. And you're right. It is silly. But it's also true. It was outside of my comfort zone. It was new, but it was also an adventure.

One thing is for sure—if my sponsor had asked me to do that call that night and then said, "Oh yeah, and by the way, in a couple years you'll train on stage at our annual convention because you'll be a top leader in the company," I would have returned my business kit and scurried back into my cozy-comfort-zone-burrow like a frightened little chipmunk. I wanted adventure, but I also wanted it at a slow pace. I needed to control my jump into this business. I wanted to learn new skills but only if I already knew I was going to be good at them before I started. I wanted to grow, but I didn't like that no one grows when things are easy. The thought of public speaking was terrifying. Being vulnerable? Nope. Sharing my flaws? No, thank you. FAILING? Absolutely not.

But here's the thing, guys: when you take little steps every single day that force you outside of your comfort zone, and little by little, step by step, you make your way up this giant mountain you never knew you could climb. Don't look at the entire mountain at the beginning of your journey. You'll hang out on the ground floor. You'll analyze the altitude and every risk along the way. You'll envision every shortcoming you possess and determine why you will stumble too much to ever make it all the way to the top. Don't get stuck in your head at base camp.

Think about the movie *Bambi*. Remember the scene where he's learning to walk? His legs splay out from underneath him and he falls down almost immediately. If you have a child of your own, you know this isn't far off from how it all starts for us humans. No one tells a toddler she has to run up a hill in 7 seconds; if that were the case, we would probably just crawl for the rest of our lives. So why do we do that to ourselves when it comes to our goals and our businesses? Why do we put pressure on ourselves and demand we know all the ins and outs and become "industry experts" on day one?

Four-and-a-half years after that training call, I hit the top of my company. During that time, I had also started working dentistry part-time and eventually fully retired. People have asked if that decision to retire was met with some push back, especially because my father, grandfather, aunt, and cousin were/are all dentists. But the truth is, I followed my gut like I have for every big decision thus far in my life. And thankfully my family respects and supports that. I listened to those "God whispers" and took my life in a different direction from where I had envisioned it going 5 years earlier when I graduated and moved to Seattle, eager to start my dental career.

A lot happened since my rise to the top with my first business. As a self-proclaimed "go with your gut" person, I moved several more times, met the man of my dreams, and we had our first child together. Having a baby changes you. Those changes can (and do) look different for everyone. For me, it inspired me to start looking into cleaner and healthier ways of living. I started switching out toxic products for cleaner labels and making healthier choices day by day. I'm a believer that everything has a purpose in your life. While my first business introduced me to the incredible industry of Network Marketing, my second business is my lifeblood.

I recently started over again, completely from the bottom. (Yes, of course it was terrifying and I was full of doubt). But I don't let doubts win—and neither do you, friends! Day 1 – zero team members and zero customers. Six months later, a team of hundreds with a customer base of thousands! How did I go from being a tippy top leader at one company to starting over from scratch and hitting the top of another company in 6 months?

UTILIZING SOCIAL MEDIA

In my former business we posted before/after photos, shared every ounce of detail you could ever want to know about a product, and spammed our friends' newsfeeds every single day. Was it effective? NO.

So how did I then start over entirely and build something larger than what I had by doing things a completely different way? Instead of sharing with you what didn't work for me, I'm going to tell you what did. It's not hard and it's not rocket science. But let me first start by saying this . . .

"Knowledge doesn't bring success—application does."

It's one thing to learn WHAT to do (which I will teach you), but it's an entirely different thing to actually apply what you've learned (and that part is up to you)!

You've probably heard of the term "personal brand" before when referring to social media. What does that even mean? Well, it means just that. It's what sets you apart from everyone else out there. Each of you reading this book has experienced a unique set of chapters in your life. It doesn't matter if you're a twin with all the exact same friends and family members as your sibling, you still have your own unique experiences that are unlike anyone else's on the planet. They are what make you special. They are what set you apart. No one else can be YOU. Every decision you make is shaping who you are and who you ultimately will become. Share these experiences with your networks on social media.

Let's do a quick exercise. Grab a pen and paper and answer these questions. How would you describe yourself? What are your interests? Hobbies? Favorite things in life? Jot down 25 words right now, things that would give a perfect stranger a pretty good idea of who you are. Got your 25? Good. Now let's narrow that down a little. Read over the list. Are there patterns? Similarities? Generalizations? Things you can bundle into a term or two? Let's condense the list down to the top 5. Take a few minutes to do this now. But actually do it. Yes, now. This book is only going to be as helpful as you allow it to be. :) This list of 5 is your "personal brand." These 5 things are what make you unique and different from others. These 5 things showcase who you are! THESE are the things you post about when you post on social media. Don't try to blend in, my darling, because you were born to shine!

Now that you understand what your overall social media presence should look like, let's talk about how to weave your business into it. No one wants to follow someone whose account is a billboard for their business. People aren't coming to social media to buy things. They are coming there for value to be added to their lives. We're selfish creatures—we want to know "what's in it for me." If your page is all about your business, with no added value for me, you'll likely be unfollowed.

Adding value is key. Ok, but HOW? What's something you can do as good or better than anyone else? Let's start there. Maybe you're really handy and can fix anything. Awesome! Go live on social media and show how you fixed the leaky faucet. Perhaps you're an excellent baker. Go live and share your recipe for the perfect cheesecake. Or maybe organization is your skillset. Share a post with your latest pantry organization hacks! Your network will love it! Pretty soon they'll start coming to your page for more how-tos. They'll be tuning into your social media and waiting for what's next. Then, when you creatively share about your business here and there, they're intrigued.

I called it "creatively sharing" because no one wants to be spammed with every detail related to your project—yawn—so boring! Again, we're selfish creatures. So you've got to share what's in it for them! Share the RESULTS people are getting by using your products. Less joint discomfort? More confidence? Feeling more healthy? It's different for every business. But discover what benefits YOUR company's products provide and start highlighting those.

Alright, so let's recap a little. You've got your personal brand. You've got your products' benefits. Now let's create a little curiosity and get your network reaching out to YOU. Let's pretend your business is a supplements company. You have a killer product that helps give people glowing skin from the inside out. How do you create enough curiosity here so that people ask questions? Do you share every ingredient, how long it lasts, and how much it costs in a post and then wait for Susie to have a burning question she needs your help answering? No. Because you already gave her all the information she needs. If she has any other questions, she can run to Google. Let's think of the opposite scenario: You post a makeup-less selfie and say something like, "since I've started using this daily vitamin, my skin is glowing like I'm in my twenties again." If you're someone who is also looking for improved skin, that will make you much more intrigued to reach out, right? You don't know what product she's using. You don't know how much it costs. You don't know all the ingredients. You just know it works for your friend.

Think of it like dating. You want to create curiosity and intrigue on the first date (if you want it to lead to a second date, that is). You don't want to share your entire life story, every fear, every failure, every dream, every desire, right? You share a little here and there and keep the curiosity building.

What is your ultimate goal here? Why are you reading this book right now? Do you want to become a top leader in your company? Great! Maybe it's not your goal to make it to the top. Maybe your goal is to earn a killer paycheck that will take stress off of your family's monthly budget and provide some fun "extras." Great!

Maybe you don't really know where you want to take this new business of yours. If that's the case, I want to challenge you to spend some time with those dreams you haven't dreamed since you were a kid. What would you do if time and money weren't an issue? Who would you help? How would you contribute to society and make the world a better place? What would your days look like from start to finish? Who would you spend your time with? There are no wrong goals here, but you need to be clear on what you want if you want to get to where you want to go.

Start taking daily steps in the direction you want to go. Do the hard work. Don't skip the events or trainings. Show up on social media. Share your wins. Share your failures. Be present. Make your presence known. Work on yourself. I learned early on that your business will never outgrow you. If your business isn't growing, it's dying. Well the same is true for you. If you aren't growing, you're dying, friends. Keep growing. Keep learning. Keep pushing today to be better than you were yesterday.

It's taken me almost 8 years of learning, growing, and evolving, and it all started with a training call. Now there are people out there asking me to share my story as a co-author in a book with Jordan Adler! WHAT? Did you know his book, *Beach Money*, was the first network marketing book I read in my first week in business? It's true. He's one of the reasons I'm where I am today, and if just one of you who reads this chapter gains value or insight from it, every single pebble, rock, pothole, and road-block I've endured along this crazy journey of entrepreneurship will have been worth it.

MOMENTUM MAKERS

1. **DON'T LOOK AT THE ENTIRE MOUNTAIN AT THE BEGINNING OF YOUR JOURNEY.** Take little steps every day that force you outside of your comfort zone and little by little you'll make your way to the top of the mountain.

2. **CREATE YOUR OWN "PERSONAL BRAND".** Describe yourself, your interests, your hobbies, and your favorite things in life—write them down! Condense the list to the top 5. These are your personal brand.

3. **POST ABOUT YOUR "PERSONAL BRAND".** Post about those things that showcase who you are and make you unique and different from others. Don't try to blend in, because you were born to shine!

4. **CREATIVELY SHARE YOUR BUSINESS HERE AND THERE ON SOCIAL MEDIA.** Share the benefits your company's products provide and the RESULTS people are getting by using these products.

5. **CREATE CURIOSITY AND INTRIGUE IN YOUR PRODUCT WITHOUT GIVING ALL THE DETAILS.** This attracts people and will have them reaching out to YOU. People will start asking you questions about your products and how to get the results they see..

JENNIFER BOUCHER

MORE THAN SKIN DEEP
IGNITING YOUR PASSION WHILE
FINDING YOUR PURPOSE

I was always looking for a better way. I never believed that we were born into a magical world like ours only to spend our lives grinding from 9-5 every day, struggling to make ends meet, and leaving this earth wholly unfulfilled. That never made sense to me, yet somehow that is what we all have become accustomed to. I didn't believe that there were just the "lucky ones," those with incredible gifts and talents or those who were born into fortune. I always knew there was more for those who may look ordinary on the outside but were capable of greatness, those of us who believe in two very important things: passion and purpose.

My first job out of college was at Memorial Sloan-Kettering Cancer Center, a fantastic place in itself. I was hired as the assistant to the Director of Development, and I really had no idea what that meant, other than I was going to be well-poised to do what I do best: help others. The first thing that struck me during orientation was I was seated between a radiologist and a member of the custodial staff. The message was we are all the same here—we are all here for the same reason. This was a beautiful entrance into the workforce at age 22 and one that likely shaped my professional persona.

In the development department we ran all of the major fundraising events for the hospital. One of our biggest days of the year was the New York City Marathon, in which the participants of our running team, known as "Fred's Team," would run to raise money for the pediatric unit.

We had bleachers set up outside of the hospital; there was a DJ and plenty of food and drink. The children who were well enough would come out to cheer on the runners; some were bundled up in wheelchairs and with IV poles. Our runners were easy to spot, dressed in purple and orange, and would come right to the bleachers to high five the kids, some handing off their medals from marathons previously completed.

It was then that I realized I was exactly where I belonged, on the front lines of volunteer work. I loathed going back to my desk to mail merge donor letters and sort auction items, but I loved taking phone calls from people looking to create funds or events in honor of their loved ones. It was the stories that I craved, combined with the chance to help take away a piece of someone's pain and put a little comfort in its place.

Whenever I told people that I finally figured out that it was my calling to be a full-time paid volunteer, they would laugh. And rightfully so because that title contradicts itself. However, I was certain that I could find a way to make it happen. Maybe I would become best friends with someone like Oprah or Angelina Jolie, someone with unlimited funds but short on time who would put me on salary to do their volunteer work around the globe! Unrealistic? Maybe. Then perhaps I would invent something so profound I would make my billions, retire at age 25, and fulfill my dream of building orphanages, saving all of the animals, and holding as many hands in hospice as I could.

I bounced around corporate America, slowly climbing the dreaded ladder, as each idea fell flatter and flatter. Once a week or so I would leave my respective office around 6:00 pm and pop into a local children's center or soup kitchen. I wasn't fulfilled; my volunteer work wasn't consistent, but I was doing my best for the time being. It wasn't until I got married and became pregnant with my first child that I was able to step away from the grind and really assess what I wanted and how I was going to make it happen. I always wanted to write a book or contribute to a weekly column, but what did I really have to say at that point, save for a bunch of entertaining anecdotes from life in the big city? My story was still unfolding, and I would need to be patient in order to garner proper interest.

Of course things only got busier and more complicated as I became a first-time mother. There was so much to learn, so much to navigate, so much to fear, yet so much to enjoy. Once again, this was not the time for me to buckle down and pen my memoir or even submit an essay to the *New York Times* "Modern Love" column (although I did try - status: rejected). But I still knew, deep down in my soul, that I was meant to live my life caring for my children from home, providing for them financially, and also helping others. I had no idea how this would come to fruition; I just knew that is what I was destined for. As a wise woman told me years later, "It's as if you have a compass in your right hand, upside down. You need to flip it over and transfer it to your left hand in order to find your way." For some reason, that made all the sense in the world to me.

It wasn't that I was chasing the wrong dream; I was just approaching it from an unnatural angle. I wanted to write the book before I had the story; I wanted to save the world before I had established my own self and my own family. I had no idea that there was a way to accomplish everything I wanted through an industry I had never even considered.

The direct sales channel is probably the last place a natural born skeptic ends up, but in the words of Jane Pratt, "It happened to me." My son was a little over a year old, and I had made copious rounds of mommy and me classes and weekly playdates, trips to parks and playgrounds, and activities. I was starting to feel that itch again, wondering if there was something more for me out there and when I would be brave enough to go get it.

As fate would have it, a friend of mine presented me with a direct sales opportunity selling skincare, just as I started asking myself, "What's next?" She had her baby 10 days before mine and was struggling with the work/life balance, one that is made even more difficult by the dreaded mom guilt—

new mom guilt, no less. I turned her down at first and swiftly, at that. After all, I was focusing on my blog that was paying me exactly zero dollars. Plus, I washed my face with Dove soap and never even thought of using so much as an eye cream. I figured I wouldn't make a good representative of the brand, but I would be a supportive friend and customer. It wasn't until she received her first paycheck that I realized there was an opportunity for real money to be made. I decided to give it a second look when my mother said, "Just try it for a year. What do you have to lose?"

I jumped in with only one foot and a slew of parameters. I wasn't "hopping on" conference calls. I wasn't doing anything that required a babysitter. I wasn't hosting parties, and I was certainly not going to let it take over my social media newsfeed. I had a cute dog, a cuter kid, and lots of witty banter for my network! You know, which was also paying me exactly zero dollars. I stuck to my guns for about 6 weeks before I realized that if anyone was going to be all in with me, I needed to be all in myself. I started listening to training calls and quickly learned that I could take advice and personalize it, rather than attempt methods that just weren't my style.

Social media soon became the perfect place to mix my cute kid/dog/witty banter with clinically proven products and snippets of how I was running a business as a stay-at-home mom of a toddler with one on the way. Friends and distant acquaintances alike started approaching me, wondering if perhaps this was something they could succeed in as well. I would echo the words of my mother and my sponsor: "Just try it." A phrase that quickly removes the pressure from most situations.

I widened my network using Facebook, Instagram, and even learned a few tricks on that dinosaur LinkedIn, such as upgrading to Premium and connecting with second-generation friends. It soon became second nature for me to ask a friend for an introduction to someone in their network who struck me as a go-getter. My brand was already in place, so people knew what to expect and found me genuine. Cute kid/dog/witty banter and now working girl with great skin? Intriguing, tell me more! However this is a very important inflection point that often separates the success stories from the Karens. You can have a huge network, a great brand, and a genuine voice and still turn people off by over-posting. Flooding your network's newsfeed with a sudden influx of your "new venture" is the quickest way to get blocked on social media. Just like I learned at Memorial Sloan-Kettering, most things worth doing are marathons and not sprints. Network marketing is no different. You must build it, work for it, and share authentically in order to create a solid foundation for success.

Fortunately, the product profile was fantastic and the pipeline was full and growing quickly. Within a year I had mastered selling product while also building a team of smart and savvy individuals who also wanted more for themselves and their families. It felt very natural to be able to encourage people to use the products when they delivered such great results, especially for someone like me who barely wore make-up. In my second year of business, I realized that I was making the same amount of money I had previously been making in pharmaceutical sales, this time from home with two small children.

My third year was pivotal in that I earned my company car, was making great money, had earned yet another luxury trip, and became pregnant with my third child. Smack in the middle of all of this good fortune, it occurred to me that giving didn't have to happen at the end of every year; maybe I could give on a more consistent basis. I had met many wonderful people in the company who were so successful that they were able to open their own orphanages, dog rescue facilities, and military spouse foundations, yet I didn't want to wait until I made my millions. I wanted to start right then and there. My issue has always been picking just one organization to donate to, but if there's one thing this business has taught me, it is to be flexible and find the positive in every situation, a skill I was not necessarily born with.

I decided to start highlighting a different charity every month on social media. I talked about why it meant so much to me and who introduced me to it; then I pledged to donate a portion of my monthly paycheck to that particular organization. After a year of choosing on my own, I opened it up to my network and asked them to shout out charities that were near and dear to their hearts. We were not only spreading awareness and raising money, but we were also connecting people who may have suffered similar pain through sickness, heartache, or loss.

Through all of this networking, I was offered a board position for a social service association in my town, and I accepted the opportunity. I learned that we had many neighbors in this upper middle class town and the surrounding areas who were going without food, electricity, and other basic needs after falling on hard times, something that could happen to any of us. This organization provides short-term and long-term solutions for these families as well as hot meals on Thanksgiving and Christmas, gifts for children at the holidays and on their birthdays, and a fully stocked food pantry for them to shop in.

My success in network marketing has allowed me to not only be there for my own family but also to be there for these local families in need, not just by donating money or collecting the food, but actually handing a father a big bag of supplies and gifts for his two-year-old girl's birthday party, one that she wouldn't have otherwise. To embrace a single mother and give her a bag full of new clothes and shoes for her 15-year-old, complete with wrapping paper and tape to provide the satisfaction of doing it herself, when life wasn't currently allowing her. These moments not only fulfilled me deeply but also showed me that my belief in a channel that I once scoffed at is actually what is making my dream come alive.

Last year I was presented with an award by the YWCA for empowering women and eliminating racism. It was called the Woman to Watch award. I have to admit, I felt quite small standing between the CEO of an organization that educates and houses troubled youth and the founder of a literacy program. I didn't have nearly as much experience as the woman who had traveled the world saving women from human trafficking situations. But as my friend put it, "You have built a team of thousands of entrepreneurs and mentored them to want more and do more for themselves. You give back every chance you get, all while raising those three amazing kids of yours. If that's not empowering women, I don't know what is."

That same year I stood on a stage in New Orleans at our national convention, speaking to thousands on the importance of believing in yourself. I stood there as a newly single mom, earning a full time salary from home, raising three young kids, and giving back as often as possible, a full circle moment for a full-time paid volunteer. I told them that 8 years ago I started this business because I had a little light burning inside of me. I called it my pilot light. It was always there, always flickering to remind me of what I wanted and needed from this world and what the world needed from me. But it required that spark to really burn bright. My network marketing business was the catalyst for this light to become an inferno. It gave me the confidence in myself to pursue what was possible; it gave me the connections to wonderful people who would encourage and help open doors for me, and it gave me the financial independence to do it all on my own terms.

MOMENTUM MAKERS

1. **SHARE AUTHENTICALLY.** Nobody wants a souped up (or watered down!) version of you. Social media is the perfect place to mix your life stories—your cute dog, your cuter kid and lots of witty banter—with proven products that you believe in.

2. **MAKE NETWORKING PART OF YOUR DAY EVEN WHEN IT DOESN'T BENEFIT YOU.** Success in network marketing allows you to not only be there for your own family, but also to be there for others. Network marketing can be the catalyst for your passion and purpose to burn brightly.

3. **APPROACH THINGS FROM A DIFFERENT ANGLE.** A different angle affords you a fresh set of eyes. "It's as if you have a compass in your right hand, upside down. You need to flip it over and transfer it to your left hand in order to find your way."

4. **BELIEVE THAT YOU ARE DESTINED FOR GREAT THINGS** Always look for a better way. If anyone is going to be all in with you, then you need to be all in yourself.

5. **NEVER QUIT ON A BAD DAY.** Most things worth doing are marathons and not sprints. You must build it, work for it, and share authentically in order to create a solid foundation for success.

NICHOLE SMITH
YOUR INFINITE AUDIENCE

Yes, North Pole is really a town and yes, I really lived and built a thriving business there. In 2012 my family arrived in North Pole, Alaska, which has a population of 2,000. Much to my dismay, it is also located approximately 300 miles from the nearest Target. My twins were not yet a year old, and I had just begun my first year homeschooling my two older daughters. My husband had recently completed his military pilot training and had just started working as an air refueling pilot for the Alaska Air National Guard. From the outside looking in, this was not the ideal time to launch a new business, but this is when the opportunity presented itself to me. And while I didn't realize it at the time, I had been preparing for this opportunity for years before I found it.

When my twins were born two and a half months early, I put my successful blogging and social media consulting career on hold. While I am certain that was the best decision for me and my family at the time, I missed it. Once we arrived in North Pole, I began to feel that familiar twinge of needing something more. I needed an outlet. I needed to use my brain, and while teaching my children to read and solve basic math problems was enjoyable, it didn't challenge me, nor did it push my creative capabilities. So when my sister sent me an email about a new Direct Sales company that was launching soon, I was intrigued. This company was going to be different, in that they were going to focus on selling and expanding primarily through the use of social media. This further peaked my interest and curiosity because my background was as a social media consultant and blogger. I fully understood the power of social media.

I also had a basic understanding of Direct Sales, as I had previously joined a company simply to have access to their products at a discount. I considered building a business with that company until I learned that they had a policy that prohibited the use of social media as a method to build a business. At that time, as a mother of two young children, I knew I would never be able to find the time to do in-home parties and build through traditional means, so I decided to let that business go. I accepted that a business that required me to leave my house several times a week would not fit into my current life situation and likely never be a business model I wanted to pursue.

The introduction of a new company that not only understood the power of social media but fully embraced it meant the full potential this industry provides was in front of me and attainable in my circumstance. I knew I had two options. Take it and jump in 100%, or let it pass by and risk looking back with regret at what could have been. My personality does not allow me to do anything part way, so I knew that if I chose to sign up, working towards success would consume me. My husband sometimes jokes that I am obsessive in nature but he also recognizes that can be a good thing. We both knew a new business would take what little free time I had, and I wouldn't be able to think of anything else. But I needed that outlet, and I had a vision of the potential of this opportunity, so I decided to dive in.

North Pole, Alaska is a small town with an even smaller amount of women who actively wear makeup; let's face it, the moose don't really care what you look like and 80% of the year you don't either. However, I understood that and developed a plan around the idea that because of social media, I was not limited by my geography. I also would not be limited by my situation as a full-time mom to four young children. While busy, most of us can find a few minutes throughout the day to focus on ourselves. As long as I wasn't required to devote a large chunk of time at once, I could piece together the time needed to build my business. I truly felt the old-school direct sales methods of in-home parties, conference room opportunity meetings, and monthly in person training excluded an entire demographic, specifically my demographic. I was a member of a group of women who were smart, creative, and ambitious, but who could not regularly leave their kids behind for in-person events. We were women full of potential with nowhere to direct it. I was also aware of another group: women who were already excelling at their roles juggling careers and motherhood but would never be able to fit in any additional weekly activities. These were the women who I wanted to introduce to the business. They were going to be the path to growing my empire and we were going to use social media to accomplish our "world dominance."

While very busy with the responsibilities of motherhood and homeschooling, I discovered that I had more down time than I had previously realized. And because of technology, I had all of the tools I needed to find women who were in similar positions to mine and who were looking for the opportunity I had to offer. I was able to build my business from my phone, while nursing my twins in the middle of the night. I could take selfies to post during nap time. I was able to communicate with other mothers who were lonely, bored, and yearning to create an income and find personal validation, while still prioritizing their roles as mothers. In the early morning hours, I could connect with prospects and customers on the East Coast. And when our company expanded internationally, I was able to build teams in the United Kingdom, Canada, Australia, Germany, and more. I achieved all of this simply by utilizing social media as a way to connect with new prospects.

Within a year, I reached the highest pay status of my company's compensation plan. By year two, my downline accounted for nearly 90% of the consultants in a now rapidly growing company. Around year three, I attended a Six Figure Earner Summit where I astounded veteran network marketers with my story of rapid success and significant income. They all wondered how I had done it when they had been in their businesses for years or even decades without achieving the same level of success. The answer was simple: Social Media.

Social Media gave me a larger audience than I ever could have had if I had needed to do individual meetings with local prospects. Platforms, such as YouTube, Facebook, blogs, Periscope, and Instagram, allowed me access to more potential team members than I ever could have found otherwise. Social media allowed me to find the demographic that had been missed by the network marketing industry and tap into potential that had previously gone unnoticed. Social media allowed my team and I to experience duplication on steroids with mind blowing rates of growth within our successline.

My demographic had been so overlooked that when I did start my business, I had no clue that there was an entire industry devoted to training network marketers and direct sellers. I didn't realize that books, CD's, websites, and conventions existed for the purpose of educating new consultants on how to build their business. Instead, I just started and did what made sense to me at the time.

One thing I knew about myself was that I was NOT a salesperson and I did not like sales people in general. I did not like being sold to or feeling like I was being pushed into buying or signing up for something I didn't truly want. So I decided to build a business by being the opposite of what I didn't like. I would not be pushy. I would not exaggerate or make big claims. I would not pressure anyone. I would simply do people the favor of sharing our fantastic products and the amazing opportunity that I had found. There were no scripts. There were no premade graphics about "joining my team." I was just sharing genuine stories, enthusiasm, and interest in helping others to feel the way I felt. I wanted the women I talked to, to know that this opportunity was there for the taking and that I was more than happy to show them the way.

At the time I didn't know that there was actually a method and a name to this strategy. Like I said, I didn't know there was an entire industry devoted to teaching direct selling practices and techniques. I just knew that I wanted to take advantage of this opportunity and that I could only be successful if I looked out for the best interests of my team members, instead of placing my own ambitions and goals ahead of theirs. This strategy for building was surprisingly successful, and I found validation in learning that I didn't have to be the stereotype that turned me, and so many others, off to salespeople. I was able to build a team by being the best version of myself and sharing something with others that brought me joy.

While my methods seemed intuitive for me, I learned that in order to train and lead my team, I needed to be able to explain and teach what I was doing to others. When people ask me how I built a downline of over one million consultants and have earned over five million dollars over the course of my 8 year career, this is the advice I give them:

1. Be you. On social media it can be easy to fall into the trap of thinking we have to fit into a mold of what we think people want to see. But in order to build a successful Network Marketing business through social media, you must be authentically yourself. People want to connect to the real you. They need to trust you. They need to want to be around you. If you are constantly trying on new identities, people won't trust you or feel like they know you. If you try to be someone else, your team will eventually see your true colors and lose faith in you as a leader. When people sign up for a company or purchase products, they are buying because of you. When I initially built my team, my company had not yet launched any products and our sign up kit had nothing to offer besides a free website and business cards. Yet people signed up. This is where I learned that people don't join a company. They join you. And my network joined me before even knowing what my business was about because they knew and trusted me. Be someone that people trust and want to follow.

2. Be the best version of you. Not everything we post on social media has to always be perfect. But there is a difference in sharing a personal struggle and complaining. You need to be real while also being positive. Showing your audience that you have hope, a positive outlook, and belief that you can overcome anything is a way to share your difficulties without alienating your potential team members and prospects. Remember that your social media page is your storefront. You wouldn't want to enter a store that was rundown, had broken windows, and was covered in graffiti. The same goes for your social media. You want to present yourself as inviting and welcoming, not as a person that is full of despair and drama.

And while we are at it, use caution when posting or commenting about politics or other controversial matters. You can have opinions, but remember that the way you express them has the potential to alienate 50% of your audience. When in doubt, walk away and limit the potential for drama or disagreements on your storefront.

3. Be consistent. Your presence on social media needs to be consistent. You can't disappear for a week because you are busy, distracted, or can't think of anything interesting to say. The way algorithms work, you are rewarded for sharing and posting regularly. Your followers/ friends/ subscribers will typically see what you post if you are consistent. If you only share something sporadically, then your posts are likely to get lost in the black hole of social media. I could try to give you the exact number of times a day to post and how often to go live and so on, but algorithms change so regularly that by the time you read this, the guidelines would be out of date. Instead, be present and pay attention to what seems to be working at the time. Different platforms "like" different types of content (videos, lives, graphics, posed pictures, candids), so take the time to customize your content for the platform you are creating it for. The same video may not work as well on Facebook as it does on YouTube. Instagrammers tend to like a certain type of picture. Also algorithms tend to "punish" any app that auto posts on multiple platforms at once. Whatever platforms you use, show up regularly. Make a schedule. You don't have to use all of them, but try to do two to three of them well.

Also, be consistent with your business. If you are constantly chasing after the next opportunity, starting up with the newest company, or changing your business, people will lose trust in you. Your audience wants to know that if they sign up with you, you will be there for them and not suddenly leave. Remember, people are buying you when they purchase your products or sign up as a distributor. Many people may watch your business for years before becoming a customer. Constantly changing companies never allows you to tap into those who are watching you long term. You don't want to be the kind of distributor where your followers joke and wonder what your next "big business" will be. Pick a company and become a lifer. Become your network's go to person for those products so you are dependable and reliable for years to come.

4. Content is crucial. Take the time to produce quality content for your social media accounts. It doesn't have to look professional, but take the time to proofread for typos. If you want to share a makeup selfie, learn how to take a picture in lighting that will showcase your work. You could go to entire seminars about content, so we won't dive deep into that now. Just remember the key is to be intentional and to take the time to do it well.

Additionally, the most important advice I can give you about content is the 80/20 rule. Your business should make up about 20% of your posts on a personal page or account. Any more and you will turn people off. Any less and people will forget what you do. You don't want to get the reputation of being a walking commercial. Continue to show people the person that you are while sprinkling in stories about your business throughout your posts.

5. Brand Yourself. After scrolling through social media or watching you for a week, your audience should know 5 key things about you. This gives you specific areas to focus your content around, but not so many that you forget what you are about. This will also allow your audience to remember you and what you are there to share with them. One of these five items should be your business while the other 4 make up the rest of who you are. If you can't clearly list or define these items, your followers won't be able to either. If you need help figuring out your brand, ask some friends (or better yet, ask on social media) what three things come to mind when they think of you. This can help you get started. My five areas are: 1. My fitness journey, 2. My family, 3. My life in Alaska, 4. My business, and 5. My mission, "to empower women" (which also plays into my role as a top leader in my business).

6. You are not there to sell. My last tip may seem hard to swallow if you are only using social media with the intent to build your business but remember that people will not want to follow you on social media if you do not bring value to their life. Be sure your posts do one of three things: 1. Entertain, 2. Inspire or 3. Educate (i.e. solve problems). Remember, most people shy away from salespeople and commercials. Instead, share the fun parts of your life. Share silly videos or stories of your kids. Share inspiring quotes or life lessons you experience. And the biggest one, focus on helping people solve their problems. Your products or your opportunity have the potential to help your audience with some problem they may have. Share these solutions with them by telling the story of what you do. Share posts of the fun you have at company conventions or incentive trips. Maybe one of your Facebook friends wishes they could travel more. Share why you love one of your favorite products; perhaps, you have a friend who has been looking for something just like that. Share how your life has improved because of your business. Maybe someone who is watching (who never comments or likes but has been "lurking" for years) is looking to create a life just like yours. You never know who needs what you have to offer. So don't be afraid to share it. It feels different than asking someone to buy or do something they don't want to do. Instead, feel empowered knowing that you are simply sharing something about your life that makes you happy. No one can argue or get annoyed about that.

As I approach ten years in network marketing I realize that social networking is the great equalizer for the industry. It removes most real or perceived barriers to success by allowing men and women to connect with a larger network of prospects and customers than ever before. They can connect whenever and wherever is most convenient without leaving home. In life most problems are figureoutable and because of social media, more problems are even easier to find solutions to. Excuses disappear as barriers to expanding networks, communication and to sharing a business have been removed. Now take these tools and tips and begin building your own success story.

MOMENTUM MAKERS

1. **NETWORK MARKETING IS MORE INCLUSIVE THAN EVER BEFORE.** Social Media allows previously neglected demographics the opportunity to build successful businesses on their own terms. No longer do we need to make significant commitments outside of the home in order to reach our goals.

2. **YOUR PROSPECT POOL IS NO LONGER LIMITED BY GEOGRAPHY.** Regardless of where you live or who you know, social media allows you to expand your network, share your company, and build your business all from the palm of your hand.

3. **ALLOW PEOPLE THE OPPORTUNITY TO GET TO KNOW YOU.** Remember that people buy into people before they buy into companies or products. Show off the best version of yourself and allow your virtual audience the opportunity to get to know you through social media.

4. **YOU DON'T HAVE TO MASTER THEM ALL.** Instead of thinking you must become perfect at all social media platforms, pick one or two to build an audience. Practice your skills, build your network and use trial and error to see what works. Technology is constantly changing and no one figures it all out over night.

JULIA LANE COOPER
USING YOUR AUTHENTIC VOICE TO BUILD A COMMUNITY

Network marketing has long been seen as "spammy" and "scammy," and is often called the dreaded "pyramid scheme." The truth is that network marketing is just what the name suggests: marketing to your network of friends, family, acquaintances, and, once you get a big enough following, perfect strangers, who happen to stumble upon you during an internet search or late-night trip down the rabbit hole. When you are a network marketer, people will find you. The question you have to ask yourself is: why should they stay with and support my business?

In my experience, when you tell someone close to you that you have started a home-based, small business the way they perceive you instantly changes. Somehow, miraculously, in front of their eyes, you have transformed from their dear friend or relative into a swindler and a thief who is only out to get them. They are immediately on the defensive wanting to watch their backs and not be fooled into buying the snake oil you are trying to offer to them.

Amazingly, the same transformation cannot be said for opening a brick and mortar store. People flock to it and recognize and applaud those who have a storefront. They commend them for their courageous leap of faith and tremendous amount of hard work. They make sure to visit the store regularly, and celebrate in all of their successes. Somehow, when you are "just" a network marketing professional who is "just" pounding the pavement online and made the intelligent decision not to have the overhead costs of a store, you're not seen in quite the same light.

I have had several "friends" stop speaking to me because they thought that I would be sales-pitchy and aggressive now that I owned my own business. They had a misconception that every time we would get together I would try to convince them to shop with me or sign up to start their own business. Of course, this couldn't be further from the truth. I love the opportunity to tell people that I own my own business. If they ask for more details, I tell them. If they want to know more, I go on. I don't try to sell anyone anything. Even when someone wants to buy something from me, I do my very best to ensure that it is a product that will work for them and they will love. I am always honest about what I have to offer, and I work closely with my clients to ensure it is right for them.

I have other friends who have told me that they're not really into what I have to offer. No problem. They are still my very good friends! The struggle of some network marketers comes when they become pushy and try to force people to do what they want them to do, rather than being our authentic selves and talking about WHY we love the products or services. By sharing our excitement about what we do and why we do it, others are more likely to listen and be receptive to what we have to offer.

And, why wouldn't they? You have a product or service that could benefit people. Maybe you saw or experienced first-hand how it could change lives and recognized that the business opportunity could do the same. You have something you fell in love with, and you want to share with those around you. Heck, you want to share it with the world. It is so critical that we share our stories, our histories, our reason for being, and our special gifts that we have to offer. Social media is the perfect place to do that.

But, sharing your story and experience can be one of the greatest personal hurdles of becoming an entrepreneur. This is especially true when your business is network marketing and you are trying to help others build a life they love. Given our culture's resistance to this industry and home-based businesses in general, it can be quite a challenge. Let's face it, putting yourself "out there" is scary. It can feel like the biggest risk of your life. In my experience, there has been one and only one standout way to overcome rejection, cut through the internet noise, and answer that question we asked at the end of the first paragraph: Why should they stay with and support my business? The answer, to me, is AUTHENTICITY.

The fact is that you will never, ever, ever, ever, ever make everyone happy. You are going to annoy some people with how you act or the tone in your voice or some other insignificant thing. Some people will always find a reason to reject everything. You are going to piss someone off because you said the wrong thing, at the wrong time, to the wrong person. You cannot help it. It is bound to happen. Even if you are practically perfect in every way, someone will find fault with you and what you are doing. All you can do is be YOU. "You" is literally the only thing you have control over, so own it! The right people, YOUR people, will find you. It may take time and a lot of word of mouth and recommendations and ads and videos that no one watches at first, but eventually they will find you.

I came from a very different career background when I first started my entrepreneurial journey using social media and network marketing. I have a BS in Chemistry, an MBA, and spent years in the pharmaceutical and food industries. Dealing with CEOs and regulatory agencies had left me married to the idea that when I wrote and spoke and presented myself that I had to be someone else. I needed to speak in a formal and scientific tone. Well, that doesn't work when you're trying to relate to people. Interpersonal connections are about, well . . . connecting. How could anyone connect to me when I spoke and acted like a robot?

I remember some of the first live videos I published on Facebook and Periscope. It sounded easy. Type a brief description, start the live video, grab an item, talk about it, and people would shop. Easy. In reality, it didn't go so well. I felt awkward and like a fraud. I didn't know these products as well as I should. I didn't understand the industry. I didn't know how to describe what I was selling in a way that I felt was compelling or that did them justice. I fumbled around. I dropped things on camera. I spoke incoherently and rambled on and on for far too long. It felt like it was a disaster.

As time went on, and with lots of practice, I began to get the hang of things. When I didn't know what to say I would talk about something else in my life: how my car battery died that afternoon, what I had for breakfast, and how this man kept riding his bike through my cul-de-sac every 3-5 minutes (we aptly named him "creepy bike guy"). I turned up the music and sang and danced along. I started being my silly self, and soon more and more people tuned in to watch, and more and more people started shopping.

I remember vividly the first time I went live on Facebook and told my origin story (those aren't just for superheroes, you know . . .) I shared about the first time I was introduced to the products I am selling now. I saw a woman use the products for the first time and transform in front of my eyes from timid and uncomfortable to open, standing taller, confident, and smiling. It was magical to watch a true Cinderella transformation, and sharing this story with my social media community brought us all closer together.

As I recounted this story on a live stream, I began to cry—on camera—in front of dozens of people who I didn't know. It wasn't a cute cry with tears in the corners of my eye, dabbed daintily with an embroidered handkerchief. My makeup did not still look amazing. Thankfully, it also wasn't quite an "ugly cry" situation with snot and boogers and sobbing. It can be easily classified as not pretty. It was raw and vulnerable and real. I thought to myself, "I am toast."

It turns out, I was so very wrong. People started commenting like crazy. They loved that I could be real and honest and show a side of me that was imperfect. Do you know what that did for me and my business? It connected people to me! It showed them who I was, and how important it was to me that I was doing what I was doing. The ones who didn't get what I was saying left. They weren't a good fit for me. Bye bye.

You know what else that did for me? It lifted a weight off of my shoulders. It made me feel alive and connected. It made me feel like a more complete person; like myself. The women I was speaking to responded to me with their stories. Now, it wasn't just me telling people how these products could change lives; it was everyone agreeing and telling their stories. And it opened the door to more connections, more conversations about more topics, and more commitment to the group of women who were all watching me together. The right people will start paying attention to what you are doing if you can be yourself. The ones who want to shop and sign up and all the things that make your business grow will eventually find their way to you.

So, here it is. It is the moment you've been waiting for this whole time. The key to success as a network marketer is to truly be your authentic self. Yep. That's it. No sneaky ways to "trick" people into buying your products. No mumbo jumbo saying "do this and get rich quick." Just be you. Be vulnerable and real with all the ups and downs of life. Talk to your network about yourself and what you're going through. Treat other humans how you want to be treated. Give and spread love and joy and kindness. Be generous with yourself, and people will come to you.

If you can be truly genuine about who you are, what you're doing, and why you're doing what you're doing, people will not only buy from you, they will buy YOU. They will want to support you. They will want to be a part of your story. Think about that for a second. Actually, stop to think about that. If you can make people feel special and give them enough of the authentic YOU to feel like they are part of your family, they will care enough about you to support you no matter what. Wow.

It is important that you also care about them. You must find authentic ways to connect with your network. Find out about them. Follow their pages. Ask about their children. Just like showing your authentic self, it is important to be authentic in your interest in your clients and your community. The easiest way to do that is to create a space where everyone can feel trust, love, and appreciation. When you foster an environment where your network can feel comfortable being who they are, you build a community of friends and clients that will never go away.

In order to do this, I created a private Facebook group in addition to my business page. My business page is used as my website, where people can find out about who I am and what we sell. My private Facebook community is where I can be open and honest with my clients, and they can connect with me. I post questions every day to find out more about them and we can have open discussions. When I am live, I talk about what is happening in my life and ask them about theirs. Frequently, we spend time just chatting, not selling and buying.

It is so essential for me to connect with my clients instead of just posting *at* them all day. I created a safe space where the women who shopped with me could feel comfortable enough to tell me their sizes and post their photos and ask the community their opinions. I built my network authentically by making new friends and letting my beautiful community shine with joy and kindness and fun and magic.

The greatest achievements in my business are the connections I have made with these amazing women, and the freedom network marketing has provided for my family. Because of my business, my husband and I both quit our jobs and have worked from home full-time for years. We paid cash for an RV and took a road trip around the country because running a successful network marketing business provided us with freedom. We saw

34 states in 6 months, met some of our amazing clients and friends that we made in our online community, and worked from the road. Our clients held shopping parties and they brought their communities into our community. It was such a fabulous opportunity to strengthen the relationships that we built in our online group.

Network marketing is more than just selling products. It is more than building a team and collecting a check from the work that you and they are doing. It is far more than just a business; it is an opportunity to connect with your clients and become friends. It is an opportunity to change the way you and your family live. It is an opportunity to build a community where people feel heard and valued. It is an opportunity to spread love and joy and support. It is an opportunity to change the world!

—— MOMENTUM MAKERS ——

1. **BE YOU!** You are the very best you that you can be. Don't be afraid to share yourself with the world!

2. **BE VULNERABLE.** Let people into your world and see the ups and occasional downs.

3. **CONNECT WITH YOUR COMMUNITY.** Don't just share at your followers; share with them. Connect by asking about and sharing in their lives.

4. **GO LIVE.** A picture speaks 1,000 words, but video says exactly what you want. It is the easiest and fastest way to share and show your community who you are.

5. **BUILD A COMMUNITY.** Create an environment that lets community members feel safe, heard, and filled with Joy and Happiness.

ERICA ANDERSON

SHARING YOUR UNIQUE SELF TO BUILD YOUR BRAND

I have always been a dreamer. My whole life, I filled my mind with big ideas of what my life would be like, never knowing what these dreams were made of or how I would get there. Maybe I'd be rich and famous or have some sort of exciting job traveling the world or saving lives. Whatever it was, it consumed me. I'd sit in my room as a kid and imagine this future life of mine, and it was good! It was sparkling; it was dazzling; it was a DREAM. And then I graduated college and entered the real world (womp). I had no big life to speak of, just an ordinary hamster wheel, corporate desk job. NOT exciting. Did I mention that I wasn't a big risk taker? Nope. My parents might as well have named me "Play It Safe Sally" because I wasn't going anywhere or doing anything that wasn't easy. I got a good job at a good place with good pay and good benefits. Sounds good, right?

As I moved along in my "career" and realized that working in the corporate world was kind of a bummer and that my big dream life wasn't going to just fall into my lap, I became a little bitter. Don't worry, I had a wicked sense of humor about it, so I think people still liked to be around me (that I know of at least), but I grew more and more restless and even more negative about my situation. Don't get me wrong, I had a GREAT life. I had a wonderful family, a loving husband, a good job, and an adorable (and active) son. But I was the definition of "unfulfilled," and I was letting the stress of my job come home with me. It was interfering with my family life. This is NOT how I wanted to live, and I just kept thinking to myself, "Is this all there is? For the next 40 years, I'm going to be doing THIS?"

I knew that I couldn't go on like this much longer; something would have to give. I even started to get chronic headaches and fatigue—all caused by the stress and anxiety of my current situation. At first I told myself to get it together, that moms do this all of the time and that they're all just fine. And between you and me, I felt a little pathetic, if we are being honest. All of these crazy emotions were ruling my world, and each day I had to deal with it. My life consisted of waking up, getting everyone ready, eating breakfast in the car, dropping off my son at daycare, sitting at my desk doing my mind-numbing work for 9 hours, picking my child up, throwing something in the microwave for dinner, putting a child to sleep, and passing out. Rinse, repeat. Every day. Some big, exciting life, huh?

When I was approached to join my company in 2014, I think I may have let out an audible "HA!" I'd been approached for these things before, and I had a bad feeling about direct selling. I was hater number ONE. I just KNEW they were all shady, cheesy, and probably illegal. What a sham! Did I mention I was a little bitter?

But after I got over the initial gut reaction of NO WAY IN HELL, I thought about it, and this time felt different. I was approached by a woman that I truly trusted. I was pretty sure she was a fairly normal human with a decent head on her shoulders. She can't be that insane, right? When I agreed to talk with her, she told me a few key things about our business that really resonated with me. The brand recognition stood out to me; plus, I'd seen the results from the products on her social media feed, so I knew the stuff worked. Could I? Dare I? I mean, what would people think?

Now, I typically overanalyze EVERYTHING. Deciding what to have for dinner is the worst part of my day. But for this, my response was an almost immediate "YES!" I had a gut feeling, and I didn't wait for my more negative side to kick in. In fact, I had silenced it altogether. I knew in my heart that this was going to be big. I knew that this could potentially change my life in the ways that I had always dreamed. I knew. So I said yes.

I was ready to make a change. I was done waiting around for something good to happen. I was ready to do something different, for goodness sake, even if it meant taking (what I thought at the time was) a risk. No more "Play It Safe Sally." This was a new Erica, one who was ready to give her all to something she knew nothing about on the chance that it could be a vehicle for change for her and her family.

I hit the ground running. I was tired of being cautious and timid. I told everyone about what I was doing, and I was so dang proud of it. I'd never before felt passionate about a job like I felt about this one. And it truly did change my life. I was able to retire from my corporate career after a year of running my Network Marketing business on the side and have been able to completely change the financial trajectory of my family's future. We've traveled the world with the company and have been on adventures of a lifetime, and I have thought, in those moments, THIS is what I was dreaming off my whole life. I've found it.

And best of all, I have changed. I have grown. I am a hopeful, positive, friendly, and supportive person. I have seen success, and I've seen failure, and I've learned from them both. I have associated myself with a community of smart, encouraging, loving, and incredible people whom I will always call friends. I cannot imagine the person I'd be today if I hadn't taken the chance on myself, then taken the necessary action to see it through.

And I can almost exclusively thank social media for my rapid growth and success. I love building my brand on social media and using that to attract the right customers and teammates to my business. It's fun to be able to get to know people and to show who you are on social media. Every day I decide what I'm going to show my network about me—my funny side, my serious side, what I love, how I struggle, what I'm passionate about. It ALL matters because it all makes up your unique self. And being open and relatable on social media is one of the biggest assets you can have to help you succeed in network marketing because people have to get to know you through your profile; you can only meet with so many people in person. And once they know you, they like you, and once they like you, they trust you. And that's where the magic happens. Even the most critical of people (hi, you're looking at one) can come to believe in what you believe in because they believe in YOU.

I've shared what I believe makes me unique and what sets me apart. I share my humor with my network. I share my struggles with them— issues with my child's behavior, asking for advice on health issues and sick parents. I've shared the things that I love in life—happy kids or a long walk through Target. And I've built relationships and created bonds over those topics via social media. Then I share my business and my products because I'm so passionate about them, and people believe in them because they feel they know me enough to believe in me.

So be open, vulnerable, and authentic. Share good times and bad because we all have them, and sharing them with your network makes you more relatable than those who only share the highlight reel. Give people a reason to root for you! Why did you start your network marketing business? Shout it from the rooftops! Was it so that you could save up for a house? Pay off debt? Treat your kids to a vacation? People need to know why, so they can get behind you and cheer for your success!

Be consistent. If you stop showing your network why you love your business, they'll think you lost interest or that you failed. They don't know what goes on in your head or behind closed doors; they only know what they see on your feed, so you have to show them what you love and why you love it!

And be confident. Be proud of what you're doing! You chose this, right? Stand tall and represent the brand and the products or services that you believe in. If you're meek and cautious about it, people may interpret that as you not believing 100% in what you're doing. We are always told to dress for the promotion that we want, right? Well, act like a leader! Act like someone who has seen wild success in your company. Think of someone that you look up to in your business and channel their energy.

Listen, it won't be easy. That I can promise you. Network marketing is a gritty business, and many will quit. But with a clear goal, open mind, and determination, you can see success. You have to have a little bit of moxie, but if you want it badly enough, you'll put in the work and find a way! If it wasn't hard, everyone would do it. It's the hard that makes it great.

MOMENTUM MAKERS

1. **USE SOCIAL MEDIA TO BUILD YOUR BRAND.** When people get to know you, they come to like you. Once they like you, they come to trust you. And once they trust you, they believe in what you're doing.

2. **SHARE ALL SIDES OF YOURSELF AND YOUR LIFE ON SOCIAL MEDIA: THE GOOD, THE BAD, THE UGLY.** Don't just share the highlight reel – people are searching for someone relatable! So be that person for them to connect with.

3. **BE OPEN, VULNERABLE AND AUTHENTIC.** Again, people will relate to you if you share your wins AND your struggles. Show that while you're happy with what you're doing, it doesn't mean that your life is perfect. This will go a long way in showing people that you're not perfect, but you are REAL.

4. **BE CONSISTENT.** Share something personal every day and share something business related a few times a week. If you stop posting about your business on social media, people will assume you've lost interest and it must not be that great!

5. **BE CONFIDENT.** Be proud of what you're doing and the company that you're representing. If you aren't confident, people may think that you're questioning the legitimacy of the brand, the product or the services that you're providing.

CRAIG SCHULZE

3 SIMPLE STRATEGIES FOR SOCIAL MEDIA MASTERY

Turning point moments in life are rarely seen coming but always defining. It's often said, "If I only I knew at (insert age) what I know now." We don't always get to see around the corners in life as they are approaching; but, looking back, those corners become defining turning points that set our course.

When I was younger, my goal was to help people achieve their fitness goals. The course I set when I was in my 20s was to open a gym. Eventually, that one gym turned into 5 and I thought I was on the track that would be my successful life. I was seeking out ways to actively build my business acumen, accumulate wisdom and forge meaningful business and personal relationships—life was set!

But, then it happened . . . the thing I did not see coming.

I was introduced to social media in its early stages and my entire outlook changed. My eyes were quickly opened to the possibilities of how social media could change the face of industry and quicken my opportunity to impact people's lives. To me it seemed the seeds of entirely new markets were being planted; so, my first instinct was to water them—and so began my transition from grinding away at multiple small businesses to flourishing as a highly mobile, sales-focused, online-based company of one. Social media now allows me to make money even while I sleep *and* help hundreds of people around the world earn a full-time living.

I've successfully kept a number of spinning plates in the air, the largest and most lucrative being my network marketing business. This success is in large part due to fusing what is perhaps the most powerful online tool (social media) with the purest form of selling (word of mouth). Leveraging social media has given me the ability to attract a growing audience and grow a vast network of both entrepreneurs and clients. I'm happy to report that being aware of all these possibilities and emerging trends allows me to make money even while I sleep *and* help hundreds of people around the world earn a full-time living.

My days are now defined by inspiring the people around me. I firmly believe that every one of us has the ability to rise above our doubts, fears, and struggles to discover a potential we never thought existed. True success isn't defined by our bank accounts but by tapping into our own hearts and guts and operating from that place. When you remove all the clutter and live your daily life as the truest version of yourself, you've then cleared a path to love, friendship, wealth, freedom, and life-affirming experiences. You've only got one shot, so what's stopping you from giving it your all?

HOW I GOT STARTED

During my fitness days, I had formed close ties with an extensive register of members. How? When a member would enter or exit the gym, conversations would naturally unfold, and over time, relationships would form. Through these conversations, I was exposed to members' stories, their goals, and their desires to better themselves. It was impossible not to become invested in helping each and every one of them improve the quality of their lives.

Instinctively, without motive or forethought, I was referring members to certain products or services. For instance, if someone was planning a trip to Tasmania, I'd recommend a town, a hotel, restaurants, and hotspots. If someone needed a chiropractor, I would send them to a local practitioner whom I firmly believed excelled at his job. In an alternate universe, the Tasmanian tourism industry would have paid me a handsome commission, but that wasn't the aim—enhancing lives was. I couldn't help but refer people to products and services that I believed in.

Entering the world of direct selling was a logical choice for me; it was an extension of what I was already doing for free in my day-to-day life. I always kept one eye on the latest developments in nutrition and self-improvement and would regularly try out new products. It didn't take long for me to realise that if I wanted to share the benefits of a particularly innovative or effective product, for instance a specific supplement, I already had a long list of potential buyers walking through the doors of my businesses every day. My members were already actively striving for their personal goals, so why not offer them products that I had discovered, researched, and swore by? It was a win-win situation.

At some point, I remember thinking that perhaps I was "born to sell." Now, I realise that selling came so naturally to me because I believed in what I was doing. I wanted to help my customers, and I believed that my products would be of benefit. When you truly believe in what you're offering, the pressures associated with selling fade into the background, and it becomes as simple as a conversation with a friend.

I wouldn't change my decision to open a handful of gyms, as the learning, lasting relationships, and experiences that I gained were invaluable. But I had a glimpse of something better, at least for me, something freeing and exciting and rewarding that made gym ownership seem constricting and static by comparison. I sold the businesses and entered the world of network marketing, and I haven't looked back since.

Network marketing is a low-risk model that allows you to leverage existing products, platforms, and infrastructure with the possibility for unlimited return on a low entry cost. If you treat it like a hobby, it will be a hobby. If you treat it like a business, it will be a business, whether you work around your other responsibilities in a part-time capacity or commit to it full time, like I did.

Choosing the right network marketing company required equal parts rigor and self-knowledge. It's not enough to select the largest and most successful company and hope for the best. I needed to take as much time as was necessary to research companies and their products and determine what aligned with my interests, passions, and beliefs. It all goes back to the word-of-mouth referring that we all do in our everyday lives; you wouldn't refer a friend to a restaurant with subpar food or one that you'd never visited, and the same logic applies to the network marketing industry.

I knew that my interests and passions would lie in the area of health and wellness. I knew that I would only recommend a product or service that was backed by scientific evidence. I knew that what I was selling needed to be reasonably priced because offering a great product meant nothing if nobody could afford it. I knew that the company needed to distribute all over the world and not just a handful of countries. I knew that ideally, what I was selling should lead to repeat business, as selling something that people would want/need to *keep* buying was far more dependable than one-off purchases. Eventually, I found a company that met and—in some cases—exceeded my expectations.

THREE TIPS — HOW SOCIAL MEDIA HELPED ME

When I think about the relationship between business and social media, the first thing that comes to mind is Reid Hoffman, the co-founder of LinkedIn, who said *"when thinking about how to deploy professional and social networking into your business, it's not really a question of if—it's a question of when."* What's so astounding about that accurate statement is that 20 years ago, social networking barely existed, and now not a single company or organisation worth its salt can flourish, let alone function, without it.

The list of takes, truths, and tactics that I employ in order to successfully leverage social media is expansive, but here are three of the most significant for those looking to grow their audience/client base.

1. Engage your followers directly and often, individually

In order to establish and develop your social media presence, it's important to nurture your existing networks in the most efficient way possible. The larger your audience becomes, the more daunting this task can be. I stay on top of this overload by separating everyone I know into five categories: boiling hot, warm, lukewarm, cold, and icy cold.

"Boiling hot" are those in your inner circle, those you consider your closest allies. Your relationship with these people is built on a foundation of mutual support, so if you believe in what you're offering, then you'd want them to have the opportunity to get in on the ground floor. You don't do any overt selling.

"Warm" are your connections, anyone with whom you've had a physical conversation. This category is ripe with opportunity because it's full of people with whom you've already formed the basis of a relationship.

Now we come to your social media audience. "Lukewarm" refers to those who are actively engaging with you and your content online. Though you might never have had a one-on-one conversation with these people, they follow and actively engage with your social media accounts. They like your posts, they comment on your content, and they are well aware of who you are and what you do.

"Cold" contacts are those to whom you are connected; however, they don't engage with your posts, and while they may follow you, they only have a passing knowledge of your existence. This category is also ripe with opportunity as you have the ability to grab their attention.

Everyone else is "icy cold." They're the 7.5 billion people who don't know you, and you don't know them. Once you reach a certain level of social media success, then who knows how many of these you can attract without even trying.

Ultimately, you want to move your social media contacts from cold to lukewarm and whenever possible and from lukewarm to warm so that you're able to engage in offline conversation. In the past, at the beginning of each year, I've surveyed my lukewarm followers and begun the process of reaching out to every single one, trying to take social media and make it more personal. I wouldn't even try to sell them anything; all I wanted to know is who they are, hear their story, and put a face with the name.

Obviously if you reach 100,000 followers, it's not practical to contact thousands upon thousands of people in an attempt to forge relationships. But broadly and philosophically speaking, the process of moving contacts up the ladder means that you're already doing what 99% of people aren't willing to do. And if you do it for long enough, you will reach the point where you've amassed so many followers that you no longer have to micromanage and can rely solely on the quality of your content, which is going to reach a large cross-section of people.

2. Give away high-value content for free

"What?" You ask. "Give away *what* for free?" It might sound counterintuitive to offer some of your best content without expecting anything immediately in return, but people want to see who you are, what you're about, and what you have to offer before they make any decisions. This doesn't mean that you don't get anything out of it, because in the long run, if you play it right, you definitely do.

In his *New York Times* bestseller *Jab, Jab, Jab, Right Hook*, world-leading entrepreneur Gary Vaynerchuk introduces the marketing concept of "jabbing" and "hooking." Basically, if you want to attract a customer, you repeatedly offer them valuable content that elicits an emotional response before finally selling. Value, value, value . . . offer. That is a win-win.

For example, I recently capitalised on the increasingly popular podcasting trend and created the One Shot Movement Podcast. Built around my philosophy of taking life by the horns and steering it in the direction of your dreams, the podcast involves interviews with some of the world's most effective and prosperous entrepreneurs. Each episode is packed with value. Analytics have revealed that not only is the content retaining audiences, but it is also leading to regularly repeated viewings. There's no catch, no pressure to purchase anything; there's no fine print that directs you to providing your credit card details. I'm not making a cent off the content in any direct way.

What I am getting out of the endeavour (other than building knowledge and helping others do the same) is a growing audience. Those who had never heard my name are now getting to know me in a personal, educational, and inspirational context. When someone receives high-value content without being asked for anything in return, his or her natural reaction is to say, "Hey, this guy is great! Let me see what else he's up to." Jab, jab, right hook—thank you, Gary Vee.

NOTE: Keep in mind that it's imperative to offer content to the right audience. In addition to the podcast, I have built the One Shot Movement Group, which is an online forum where those who have connected with my content can interact both with me and with each other. By offering consistent, quality content, I've attracted a true following comprised of the right audience, increasing my influence and building mutual trust in the process.

3. Develop an eye for trends and how to leverage them

In my early 20s, my first business advisor taught me a concept that I still use on a daily basis: leverage. I look for any opportunity to leverage time, money, and meaningful relationships, and both social networking and network marketing allow me to create leverage in a highly efficient fashion.

The social media landscape is constantly offering new opportunities for leverage. New platforms are emerging every other week. Even with Facebook and YouTube, the next big thing is always just around the corner (just look at TikTok and Twitch). Getting in during the early days of a platform's success can be of great benefit to your business or personal brand. Cultivating the ability to put yourself in the audience's shoes and predict how a new platform or method of content creation will fare is a highly beneficial skill.

Let's not mince words, though; the online entrepreneurial industry is highly competitive, but I recommend you use the competition to motivate you! Push yourself and tap into a spirit of innovation and ingenuity. If a new social media platform catches your eye, ask yourself why and whether or not you can capitalize on it. Will it help you deliver valuable content in new and interesting ways? Will audiences respond to its method of content delivery? How would you respond to it? Asking yourself these questions and visualising potential trends will give you a leg up and help you grow your brand exponentially.

HOW NETWORK MARKETING CHANGED MY LIFE

It's safe to say that I can separate my life thus far into two eras: before and after discovering network marketing. Before I entered the industry, I was working 12-14-hour days, darting between gyms, and facing responsibilities and issues on all fronts, then heading home and tending to administration or reading and researching. I barely had time for anyone outside the gym, let alone myself. While I was doing reasonably well and feeling fairly rewarded by helping people get fit and healthy, I was burning the candle at both ends. The more I neglected my appetite for freedom, travel, and experience, the more it grew and the harder it was to ignore.

After discovering network marketing, I was opened up to the world and all it had to offer. I was able to work when I wanted. I had more time to spend with my wife, my kids, and my mates. I was able to travel the world, meeting interesting people and having invaluable experiences. In a relatively short amount of time, I was able to grow my income in a way that would have taken decades via gym ownership. This isn't to say that hard work isn't required. It is, but that hard work is far more concentrated and efficient. Instead of grinding for hours on end each day for the same bottom line, I make effective moves at specific moments and spend the time in between enjoying life, which is why we all work hard, isn't it? We all want to have the ability to enjoy life.

But perhaps network marketing's greatest reward is that it's made me a better person. Achieving financial freedom, meeting and helping people from all backgrounds, accumulating life experiences, and being able to incorporate leisure into my routine have, in combination, led to me becoming more well-rounded, more compassionate, and wiser. I am a better father, husband, friend, and a more energetic, open-hearted human.

Network marketing has had such a profound effect on my inner and outer life that my attention is no longer on the man in the mirror but on other people. My ultimate goal is now to inspire as many people as possible to live with passion and purpose. I know how living in such a way feels— it's incredible, and it pains me to see just how many people settle for less.

If you think you don't deserve anything more, you're wrong. I'm here to tell, no, SHOW people how it can be done—how we can make something amazing out of our one shot at life. Starting now.

MOMENTUM MAKERS

1. **ENGAGE YOUR FOLLOWERS DIRECTLY AND OFTEN, INDIVIDUALLY.** It's important to nurture your existing networks in the most efficient way possible. The larger your audience becomes, the more daunting this task can be. Stay on top of this overload by separating everyone you know into five categories: boiling hot, warm, lukewarm, cold, and icy cold. You want to move your social media contacts from cold to lukewarm and whenever possible and from lukewarm to warm so that you're able to engage in offline conversation.

2. **GIVE AWAY HIGH-VALUE CONTENT FOR FREE.** It might sound counterintuitive to offer some of your best content without expecting anything immediately in return, but people want to see who you are, what you're about, and what you have to offer before they make any decisions. This doesn't mean that you don't get anything out of it, because in the long run, if you play it right, you definitely do.

3. **DEVELOP AN EYE FOR TRENDS AND HOW TO LEVERAGE THEM.** Look for any opportunity to leverage time, money, and meaningful relationships. Both social networking and network marketing allow you to create leverage in a highly efficient fashion. Look at new platforms that are emerging. If a new social media platform catches your eye, ask yourself why and whether or not you can capitalize on it. If you can, get on it

IF AT FIRST YOU DON'T SUCCEED, TRY THIS!

I was just 8 years old when my experience with direct sales started. A sweet lady selling makeup would come visit my mom, and I would get so excited to see her car pull in the driveway. I would watch anxiously as she would unload the big pink and white polka dot trunk; it reminded me of a suitcase full of wonder. To my younger self, this trunk was better than the candy store!

Inside the trunk were bags of colorful and sparkly treasures. I was mesmerized by all the vibrant shades of reds, pinks, and purples. The tiny, little lipstick samples given to me by the "makeup dealer" really secured my love for her more than anything. I was in heaven, spending hours in my room perfecting my application and lying on the floor with the catalog she gave me, circling all my "must haves." At that time, I didn't know what she was doing was even a job. I just thought it was a bunch of ladies who loved to get together, laugh, talk, and share their love of makeup. It didn't matter, really; I was ALL IN!

Fast forward 20 years and I still had no real understanding of what Network Marketing was. I attended a few makeup or spa parties, where I was now finally old enough to buy ALL the makeup I wanted. I *still* loved everything about them! I was having so much fun, and I wanted badly to be a part of this makeup loving community, BUT (there's always a "but") I was afraid I didn't know enough people to keep the parties going. I thought I would fizzle out after I bribed a few of my friends into hosting a party.

The thought of speaking to strangers gave this introverted girl who can't carry a tune the same level of anxiety as if she was about to perform on stage at the Grammys.

After college I had gotten a typical 9-5 job, but I never felt truly fulfilled or inspired by my work. Not to mention, I never felt like I was paid my worth. I didn't want to seem ungrateful; after all, I was happy to be gainfully employed. I hustled my way up the corporate ladder, but I always knew I was capable of more. I felt stuck. I felt chained to my desk and tied to a schedule that wasn't my own, my creativity stifled and passion dwindling. Even worse, little by little I began to lose parts of myself.

Enter Facebook. One day I saw a friend's post about some new magical mascara. "What in the world was she doing?" I wondered. I saw her creating mascara party event after mascara party event after mascara party event on Facebook. She was CRUSHING IT! I saw people posting pictures. Oh how excited they were to use the product and share their results. That most definitely caught my attention! For years, my fear was about doing in home parties. The fact I could now hold online parties on Facebook from my home . . . this was a GAME CHANGER. Furthermore, it was a DREAM for my introverted self!

I signed up right away and hit the ground running full speed! I had no clue what I was doing, but I was PUMPED to be creating posts and hosting online Facebook parties. Every time I would receive an email confirmation for an order, it felt like the equivalent of my winning the lottery. Well, it was not like winning the Powerball but maybe winning a solid scratch off win. My passion, my creativity, and my excitement were BACK! When an excited customer would message me or tag me in a post, it would make my whole day! For the first time, I understood what it's like to really love your work, and the extra money was pretty sweet, too! It was so exciting to be able to control my income and to be able to work toward paying off debt, save for vacations, or splurge on a nice dinner.

After about 5 or 6 months, though, something happened. I ran out of friends to host online parties. It became harder and harder to book online private parties, and my current customers were well stocked from their last few orders. Those order confirmations, along with my excitement, started to dwindle down to almost zero. Until finally, I became . . . inactive. Well dang. Now what? I had really put myself out there to be judged by the world. I took a chance, and I FAILED. I wanted to hide under a rock and pretend none of it ever happened. That would have been the easiest thing to do because I was embarrassed. I was worried that all "those people" had been right. You know, the people who tried to "warn" me that my chances of success would be slim—I mean, it's a total pyramid scheme, right? HA! You want to know something? What other people think about me is NONE of my business. That was a hard concept to embrace. I decided at that moment to take my power back and not to give others the ability to determine my happiness or the power to decide what my limits are. That was such a freeing moment, and it put me back in control. Plus, I don't like to lose. Just ask my sweet husband—he refuses to play Monopoly or other board games with me.

I decided I was going to get back on the horse and try again! After all, failure is never fatal. It's a great opportunity to learn and grow. Shortly after making this decision, though, life at home changed in a major way. My husband took a new job out of town, and we moved several hours away. We left behind all of our friends, comforts, and routines. We started over. Now, I am someone who struggles with change. I like consistency and routine. I'm the girl who still thinks her Lisa Frank trapper keeper from the 90's is an acceptable accessory to bring to important business meetings and was upset when I realized the book *Who Moved the Cheese* was not about fondue. Needless to say, I had a hard time adjusting to this big life change. The one bright spot in the move was that I got to take a break from the corporate life. I was able to fulfill a dream of mine and be home with my two little ones. I really enjoyed not feeling so rushed, and I spent my days going to the park, cooking dinner, and literally stopping to smell the roses, but eventually the internal struggle began. I loved being home and being a full-time mom, but I really missed that sense of accomplishment I got from working and crushing goals. I missed my creative outlet.

That's when I started with my second Network Marketing company. My goal this time was to take lessons learned from my first experience and come up with a strategic plan to make this successful. The same feelings of excitement and joy were back! Excited to get to work, I would spring out of bed at 5 am. I grew that business very quickly and achieved the success I longed for during my time with my first company. I absolutely loved it. As time went on, however, I started to realize it wasn't the right opportunity for me. While I learned a lot and was finding solid success, it was taking all of my time. The energy and efforts were so intense. I worked upwards of 80 hours a week and started to miss play dates, family dinners, and quality time with my friends and family. I knew something would have to change, and this was not where I was meant to be.

I started researching companies and found a new opportunity. The first two companies taught me a lot about what I did and did not want from an opportunity; they were crucial experiences and stepping stones to where I am today. Then, I found my current company. You know what they say? Third time is a charm! I saw the potential and the value in this company. I was obsessed with the product and hit the ground running! I was so genuinely excited about it; I shouted it from the rooftops, told everyone who would listen, and was promoted to an executive level of the compensation plan in just 4 months. Guess what?! All of this was done online using social media, a shy girl's dream.

Following is a breakdown of three key ways I built that momentum and some important social media lessons I've learned along the way.

1. Change your mind-set about "Social Media." From this point forward, I want you to start looking at it as "Business Media." Yes, it's a fun place to post pictures of your insanely adorable kids or that delish dinner you cooked, but you must be intentional with it. Before you make a post, ask yourself, "What's in it for my audience?" Give them value and content. Show up for them every day. This will help them get to know you, trust you, like you, and count on you. If you want to post a picture of that delicious dinner, put some content and value behind it. You could say, "This dinner knocked my socks off tonight, and my kids, who are picky eaters, gobbled it up! Message me, and I'll be happy to share the recipe." I'm providing them value, and when they message me, it gives me a chance to connect with them and really get to know them! It allows me to ask them open-ended questions and build a genuine connection.

They say the way to be interesting to others is to be interested in others. Do you sometimes feel like you're not getting the engagement on the things you post? When you feel like that, ask yourself: Have I been engaging with my audience? Have I been interacting on their posts? Have I shown any interest in them?

2. Make the Algorithms your friend! We've all heard the term ALGORITHM, probably from your Rubik's Cube. For many, this can be a scary word that is out to destroy online businesses, but that's not the case. Think about a time you were swimming in the ocean, soaking up the sun, and living your best life . . . Then you suddenly looked up and realized you were really far from the shore. You started to panic and swim to get back to shore, but the currents were too strong, and no matter how hard you swam, you weren't making progress swimming against the current. You could only fight the current for so long before you got tired and worn out. Now, what would happen if you were to stop fighting the current, swim parallel to the shore, and go with it? You'd find it's much easier, and you don't have to exert so much energy. Algorithms work the same way. If we just stop fighting them, we can use them to connect with our customers and grow our community online.

Facebook loves when you spend time on their platform, and they prioritize posts made by friends. They love when you are an active community member and especially love when you create content! Remember, ask yourself: What's in it for my audience? Does my post Engage? Inspire? Entertain? Educate?

Did you know that if you comment on a friend's post and that friend comments back, Facebook does a little happy dance and says "Yay, a genuine connection, these two are besties! Let me start showing them more of each other's content!" Wishing someone "Happy Birthday" is a great way to connect to someone you might not have spoken to in a while. Facebook really loves it when you "love" or "react" to posts; "like" doesn't excite the algorithm like "love" or "wow," so keep that in mind when you are engaging.

Creating authentic connections is key. Friend request your best customers/clients, take the time to engage with them and get to know them, build the relationship, and do the work. There are NO short cuts here. Some of my clients are now my nearest and dearest friends, and I can tell you about their lives, their kids, their pets, birthdays, etc.

Do NOT, and I will repeat this because its important, do NOT friend request people with the intention of adding them to your VIP group, sending them a request to like your page or, even worse, send them a personal message to try your product or your company. This NEVER WORKS. It's inauthentic and definitely won't build any relationships.

Also think about the medium of what you are posting. Post your own video. I love to turn pictures into a quick video, and I'm a huge fan of the Boomerang and Lumyer app. Be careful of posting outside links, such as YouTube or other external websites. Facebook doesn't like when you link people off the platform, and doing so will decrease the visibility of your post.

Go live! Live video is an amazing way to connect with your customers. When I coach my team into going live, so many of them look at me terrified, like they would rather do a Polar Plunge and jump into 40-degree water than push that little live button, and I completely get where they are coming from. As someone who used to be pretty introverted, five minutes before I was about to go live for the first time, I broke out into actual hives, my cheeks turned bright red, my neck turned blotchy, and I might have almost thrown up. True story! So instead, I created a super top-secret Facebook group with just myself in it and I went through the process! I pushed the button, talked to myself for a few minutes, and took the fear out of it! Having that run through was great practice, and I decided that I was now ready, bright red cheeks and all! Once I was live and people were commenting and interacting, it was an absolute blast! I hear this same feedback from my team members once they finally go live for the first time. My best advice is this: create a practice group to help take the fear out of it. Remember, you are talking to friends who are there to support you. Don't expect perfection; aim for progress. Your first few videos probably won't be that great, and that's OKAY! You will get better with practice. You didn't learn to ride a bike flawlessly the first time you started pedaling, but with a little practice you'll be doing sweet jumps in no time.

"BE BRIGHT." Be the bright spot in someone's day! What does that mean? ALWAYS be positive. Leave the posts about not feeling well, having a rough day, stressing out, being wronged, politics, and other controversial topics to a phone convo with your best friend. We ALL have those days, but it's important to keep it off social media.

We all have moments where we go to make a post and we aren't feeling particularly inspired or uplifting, but please do it anyway. Being positive is a muscle that you can strengthen. Think about how sometimes you dread going to the gym and you somehow find the motivation and energy to drag yourself there against your free will. How much better do you feel after your work out? I bet you never regret a great work out. The same thing applies to social media. When you are feeling overwhelmed and not particularly uplifting, take a pause and replace that negative thought with a positive one. Did you know it takes 5 positive thoughts to offset 1 negative one? Of course, it will be hard at first, but like any muscle you work to develop, it will start to strengthen.

This is especially important if you are a leader or want to become a leader. People are WATCHING your every move. Even if they aren't interacting, they are watching. People pick their leaders based on who they feel they can trust. When you are being a light, that will, in turn, draw people to you. You know that old saying "your vibe attracts your tribe"? Think about that when you think about the kind of business you want to build.

3. Demonstrate gratitude. Roy T. Bennett once said, "Start each day with a positive thought and a grateful heart." Network marketing is no different than any other business. Life as an entrepreneur has its ups and downs. It's a rollercoaster ride; you won't want to miss, but you'll definitely want to strap in and secure yourself in the seat because it is wild ride.

I want you to be really honest with yourself. How are you spending your days? Do you spend your days focusing on the things you don't want? Focusing on what is frustrating you? What you don't like? What you wish was different? Are you frustrated because sales are down? Are you upset because your team isn't performing like you want them to? Are you disappointed in a product launch from your company? Do you feel all of this is prohibiting you from being successful? Where energy goes, energy grows. If you're focusing on frustration, you are going to feel and experience more defeat. I challenge you to make a conscious effort to make a mindset shift! When those thoughts start to creep in your head, stop them and focus on what you DO want and where you want to go. Stop and think about all the remarkable things that are going right! The more you focus on that, the more wonderful things will start to show up. I'm not saying this will be easy, and it definitely takes practice, but the more you practice the stronger your muscle will become. Keep a notebook and pen by your bed and every night before you go to sleep write down 5-10 things you are grateful for from that day. I can guarantee your perspective will shift and your business will grow.

Show up every day. Believe in yourself. Be uniquely you.

MOMENTUM MAKERS

1. **TAKE YOUR POWER BACK!** Do not give others the ability to determine your happiness or the power to decide your limits. This is up to you!

2. **FAILURE IS NEVER FATAL!** If at first you don't succeed, try, try, try again! Failure is where you will gain experience, resilience and knowledge to help you continue to grow.

3. **BUSINESS MEDIA.** Change your mindset around social media. Be intentional with it. Instead of getting lost on social media for hours and posting cute puppy or cat memes, moving forward start thinking of it as business media. Business media is a BUSINESS TOOL to use to help your business grow. You will do this by providing your audience value and consistency. Show up for your audience every day.

4. **HAVE AN ATTITUDE OF GRATITUDE.** Where energy goes, energy grows. Focus on what you DO want and what is going RIGHT. Celebrate the small wins, they add up to big accomplishments.

5. **SHOW UP EVERY DAY!** Consistency is key.

NICI HINKEL

BE A DREAMER
WITH A PLAN OF ACTION

My story began long before I had any faith in the network marketing industry. I was that stay-at-home mom who was always juggling 10 different side hustles at any given time. You might know her, maybe you are her. I was a math tutor, a post-partum doula, and a housecleaner for a friend. I sewed baby clothes and embroidered shirts and backpacks. I was an extreme couponer, and I hoarded toothpaste and deodorant I got for free with coupons. Anything that I thought would improve our finances, I tried.

From the outside looking in, however, we weren't broke by any means, just your average family. My husband was an airline pilot for a regional airline and had a solid good job; however, being married to a pilot who travels for a living is not always easy. We moved away from our friends and family in Oklahoma to a perfect little suburban town in South Texas to be closer to his job. We had 4 children over the span of 6 years while living far from family and with almost zero help. Our oldest was 7 when I was introduced to my current company, and my youngest was only one.

As you can imagine, with that many small people in my home and a husband who travels for a living, my life was complete chaos. We had no family to help, and financially, there was no way we could have hired help for me. I was searching for some meaning and a way to have extra cash, so that I could put my girls in ballet some day and sign my son up for peewee football. The extras were things we couldn't do at the time because we were just a typical, average, young family who was living paycheck to paycheck. I was desperate for some relief not just financially, but to help me keep my head above water.

I had tried network marketing several times before I found my current company, but I never saw it as a real way to make income. It was more to get free products, and I always walked away breaking even or slightly in debt, but even still it felt like a success because I got all these free products! I always looked at the people at the top of these companies more as celebrities. They were a status I didn't quite think I could achieve and had never even strived towards. Right before starting with my company, I had joined another company selling jeans with my best friend, and we jumped into this one because we were jean hoarders. Designer jeans at a discount—sign me up!

That year our "celebrity leader" continued to push the need to go to a convention in Vegas, so my best friend Heather and I decided—let's do it—girl's trip! We had never gone on a girl's trip together. Because I had 4 small babies at home, all I could sacrifice was one night away, so we found cheap tickets and made the plans. Right before the convention, they set a goal for us: if we sold so many pairs of jeans, we got to go on stage and earn extra cash. I love a good challenge, so I set my mind to it and went to work. It was the smallest convention ever, but I got to walk up on stage and was handed an envelope full of cash in front of a few hundred people, and that was the moment I realized, maybe those top leaders aren't really celebrities. Maybe, it's not out of reach. Sadly, shortly after, the company went out of business; but that was the moment my eyes were opened to the possibilities in network marketing.

While my personality on the outside is very carefree and scattered, I have a very analytical mind, and I got my degree in math. I am truly an odd mix of talents, and you would never know at first conversation that I'm a math nerd. I can be the biggest ditz on the planet, and I do brilliant things like lose my phone while I'm talking on it or try and open my front door with my car fob. But I love analyzing numbers and data. I might just be able to solve all of the world's problems, or at least all of my own problems, in an excel spreadsheet.

So after I saw a little glimpse of the vision of network marketing as that company was shutting down, my same best friend joined the company I'm with now. She joined it to lose weight, like 99% of the others who do. But my mind wasn't on weight or health at the time; my gears were turning onto the possibility of something better for those 4 tiny babies of mine.

I'm a dreamer by nature, and I jump into almost everything with both feet, without much hesitation. So in fine Nici fashion, the first thing I asked of Heather was for her to send me the compensation plan. I didn't want free products this time; I was ready for more. I was ready to stop all the side hustles and extreme couponing. She didn't even know where to find the compensation plan, but eventually, she got it to me. And I opened up my excel spreadsheet, and I went to work crunching some numbers. And my mind was blown. I knew right there, I'm doing this. I was giddy with excitement as I joined that day and got to work.

I set an initial goal to pay for my groceries, so I could quit tutoring. Groceries for 6 people add up, and I thought that was a lofty goal. I also wanted to go on one date a month with my husband. We had not been on an official date but maybe three times since having children, and I needed some fun back in my life. I had the numbers laid out and a plan in place, and I fully expected it to take a year or two to reach that. Because network marketing is hard, right? I remember talking on the phone to an old friend who was making over 6 figures with another network marketing company and thinking with a glimmer of hope, "Wow, that would be insanity!" I knew this wasn't going to be fast money, and I knew getting to the top was going to require work, but I was all in. I jumped in immediately, sharing about what I was doing and being vulnerable with why our family needed this on Facebook, and I was overwhelmed with the positive response I got back.

I'll never forget the day my belief became solid. This could provide me and my family endless possibilities, and I didn't have to be that "celebrity" to achieve them. The possibility was no longer insanity. I had just had lunch with a friend and was sitting in the parking lot before I headed home. I was checking my back office, and I saw that my paycheck had posted. I had hit my goal. It was 3 months in, and I had already earned enough to pay for our groceries and some extra. I'll never forget sitting there with tears falling down my face and realizing I had totally put God in a box on what this could do for our family. I really thought I was dreaming big. That was the moment I dropped any preconceived notions of how high this could go and realized this was going to be so much bigger than I ever could imagine. And on top of that, I was falling in love with the products, so my vision was growing to so much more than just financial freedom. I was building something real.

I could continue this story and tell you all the glamorous things that happened to me after my business took off: 5 shopping sprees, 7 free trips to Hawaii, a new Lexus 5 different times, countless prizes, and rising income. But I want you to know, there's so much more to this industry than the glamour we see from the top earners. I was a stay-at-home mom to 4 small children who just wanted to pay for her groceries, and a few years later, I was leading a team of over 20k people. For any normal human being, this takes GROWTH. There's so many mistakes I've made along the way, and so many balls I've dropped while trying to balance way more than I could hold. But I wanted to share a few things I did do right while building my business on social media and a few lessons I learned along the way.

Growing a network marketing business on social media at first glance can seem so easy. We have thousands of people at our fingertips, and it takes one press of the button to share with them. It feels like there are no consequences behind our computer screens when we copy and paste another post someone made and press send. Easy peasy, right? It really can be, but there's major groundwork that must be laid beforehand to make this work.

TRUE TO YOURSELF

First and foremost, you must know who you are and be true to yourself. The masses have joined the world of social media for connection. They are not there to buy a product. They are not there to join a business. They are there for connection. And there's only one real way to give someone true connection, and that's to be completely and radically vulnerable and authentic.

If you are reading this and thinking of jumping into network marketing, I really challenge you to take a good look at your feeds on social media and ask yourself, "Is this who I am??" Attraction marketing is probably a buzzword you've heard a million times, and it can and does work, but portraying yourself as attractive isn't how it works. I like to think about the people I admire the most and who I look up to. They are not perfect by any means, and I'm actually very aware of their weaknesses. Now, I'm not aware of all their negative emotions, just their weaknesses. If you portray yourself with no faults, it's not relatable; however, if you portray yourself with constant negative emotions, it's toxic. So be very aware there's a big difference between the two.

Social media should be fun, and you should also be there with the primary goal of connection. Are you painting a picture of yourself that is honest and real? The only real way to connect with someone is through honesty. This can be scary, and it can be vulnerable to put yourself out there in this way, knowing that not everyone may like who you are. But that's ok. You can't control that. To get true connection through social media, you have to show us who you are, openly and honestly.

THE SOCIAL BRAND

I want you to choose 2-3 things about your personality that you love, that's where you will find your brand, make that your focus. Are you orderly and great at structure? Or fun loving and a hot mess? Both are great and needed in this world, but don't try and portray yourself as orderly and put together if you are the hot mess. (I am!) BeautifulSweetDisaster is actually my Instagram handle because I am such a mess, but I love that about myself because I can show my audience there is beauty in imperfection and the world needs people like us, just like we need people who naturally have it all together. If you do naturally have it all together, don't be ashamed of that and use that to share with us hot messes all your secret life hacks. We need each other. Make sharing your journey in network marketing fun and true to who you are, and you will see a crazy different response than if you are only copying and pasting ads without revealing your heart.

In branding yourself, it's also important that your brand fits your company. If one of the things about yourself is your love for soda and candy and you are in the health and wellness industry, you might have a hard time attracting your audience to what you are selling. Make sure one of the things you are choosing to brand yourself with is going to attract the same audience who would be interested in your product. It also gives your audience trust in you and let's them know that you do believe in what you are promoting and not just promoting it to earn fast cash.

YOU MUST WORK IT

It's also very important to be intentional. Alec Clark said, "You can work your business part time, but you cannot work it part of the time." And this statement is so true when it comes to being successful, no matter what success looks like for you. If you are sporadic in how you post and share, you will not get traction. If you are devoting 5 hours a week to sharing and branding on social media and you try and do all 5 hours in one day, you will get a very different response than if you spread that out and do 5 hours over 5 days. So create a plan for yourself, so that you don't fall into this trap of only sharing and working part of the time.

For my team who is interested in the business part time, I have made them a 5-hour workweek checklist. It breaks their week into 4 days of work with one longer 2 hour day that includes planning their week and 3 one-hour days. Some of the things included in this checklist are making connections on social media, commenting and engaging on posts, reaching out and having genuine conversations with new people, following up with prospects, and sharing your product on social media. You truly can grow a lasting residual business but you have to be intentional in doing so and don't just expect it to happen to you. I promise, your top leaders did not just get to their rank by happenstance. They had a vision and they saw it to fruition. You can too!

THE FORMULA

I break my posts into two types – branding and business. I aim for health and happiness. These posts are generic posts about health, who I am, and my life, and I try and give back to my audience in some way. Do you ever read someone's post and feel excited that you learned something new? Not just learned a fact about health, but something tangible that you can put to use immediately. If you can give your audience something like that, they will keep coming back for more. Do you love to cook? Don't just show them pictures of your food, show them how you made it! Are you great at hair and makeup? Give short and easy tutorials and tips! Even humor is a great way to give back. If you can be a ditz and do hysterically dumb things like try and open your door with a car fob or lose your phone and find it in the freezer, instead of getting down on yourself, poke fun at it! Because guess what, you are not alone. Most of us moms juggling too much tend to do brainless things, and it is a great way to build that connection with others when they know they aren't the only ones.

Every week on the first day of the week, I sit down and plan my posts for that week and make 3-4 of them branding/generic content posts and 3-4 of them about my business. Make sure your business posts are personal and use your voice; make sure they don't become an advertisement. Again, give back in these posts too. Share how your product is helping you and give your audience fun tips. Put your face in as many of your business posts as possible, so that it's you and not just your product they are seeing. Remember, you are building connection and trust, not selling a product. The product sale happens naturally because the connection and need for what you have to offer is there. Planning ahead will be a game changer for you if you are intentional and sit down and do this. If not, it's easy to let time slip and look up and realize you haven't devoted any efforts to building your brand or business on social media and find yourself as a "part of the time" worker again. So be intentional and plan ahead.

And last, don't get caught up in the numbers game. Building your following can be helpful, but it's way more important to interact and build influence with the following you already have. You do not need a million Instagram followers or even a thousand to be able to build a successful business. Take a deep breath and just jump in with what you have. Have fun with it, be relatable, and be yourself.

I've been with my company for over 7 years now, and it is so humbling to look back on how far we have come. Both my husband and I have gotten to the top ranks in our company. Our kids are no longer babies, and we have been able to give them all we dreamed of and so much more. I've been able to get the help I needed, so that I no longer feel like I'm just barely keeping my head above water, and my husband quit flying for the airlines, pursued a different passion of his, and is able to work from home.

It seems crazy when I look back on my initial goal of grocery money and one date a month with my husband. This industry can completely change the trajectory of your life, like it has ours, and I'm so excited for you to be on this journey. Have an unwavering belief that this is possible for you, and this story can be yours. You can set small goals to reach for in the beginning, but don't start off by putting God in a box the way I did, DREAM BIG! Like bigger than you could ever imagine, and definitely bigger than grocery money. It's not about buying our dream home or fun vacations, those are great, but it's so much more. It's creating a lasting legacy. It's a legacy not just for me and my children, but for their children too. What we have built with this business is changing future generations in my family, and for that I will be forever grateful for this opportunity.

MOMENTUM MAKERS

1. **BE YOURSELF AND MAKE CONNECTIONS.** People join social media to make real connections with people they trust. This is why being vulnerable and authentic is vital. So make sure you are presenting your true self and you are connecting with people daily and not just using your platform to sell a product.

2. **CHOOSE YOUR BRAND.** Choose 2-3 things that are true to who you are, and make the majority of your posts focus on those things. Also make sure those things complement the product you are sharing and that they don't contradict each other.

3. **BE INTENTIONAL AND EXPECT TO PUT IN TIME.** Make sure you are carving time in 4-5 days a week to work your business. That might just be an hour each day or it might be 8 hours. Either way – guard that time and have a written plan so that you will use every second wisely!

4. **GIVE BACK ON SOCIAL MEDIA.** This is key to building trust and likeability. Make sure at least half of your posts are giving your audience something. Maybe you are teaching them a recipe, making them laugh, or sharing a product review. Regardless, you want your audience to walk away wanting to hear more from you.

5. **HAVE A PLAN.** Plan what you are going to post on social media a week or a month ahead. This way you are sharing about your business regularly and intentionally and not sporadically with little thought. Of course, I still make posts sporadically about my life – but I also have a very strategic plan.

6. **BE A DREAMER!** This industry is made for dreamers. So Dream Big!

SHAWN AND MICHELLE POE
FREE RANGE HUMANS

"Michelle, you're entrepreneurial. You're passionate about people, and you're passionate about health! You need to take a look at this ABC Investigative Report!"

Little did Shawn and Michelle Poe know that one message through FB messenger, which eventually led to a meeting they went to in 2011, would change everything, surprising even the person who invited them to the meeting who had no idea of everything happening behind closed doors. NEVER prejudge anyone in your network because they may be the very people praying at night for something to change, for something different to come into their lives. Three separate hardships were hanging over Shawn and Michelle, one health-related and two job-related.

Shortly after their first daughter, Calista, was born, Michelle started to experience tingling on the side of her face, almost like electric pulses. Very quickly, this expanded to half her mouth and the top of her head. The progression was rapid and painful, but she always put on a smile when needed, and hardly anyone outside their close family knew anything was wrong.

We will never forget one night when it was so painful for Michelle we needed to head to the ER. After what seemed like an eternity of the doctors running test after test, one physician came to the waiting room for an update and informed us they might have to do exploratory brain surgery or, as he so eloquently put it, "crack open her head" to figure out what was going on and that it may be a tumor or brain cancer. Scared, nervous, and helpless don't even begin to describe the feelings we both had. Michelle's health continued to decline, leading at times to limited mobility of one side of her body, including her arm and leg, eventually sliding into issues with vision and hearing on that side as well.

Shawn came home from work one day to find Michelle sitting in a rocking chair with their daughter in her arms and tears rolling down her cheek. When asked what was wrong, Michelle said she was imagining their daughter Calista growing up without a mom, missing her graduation and wedding, and Shawn having to raise her as a single dad.

Michelle's health continued to impact their lives every single day. She had seen some of the best doctors in the world from the Mayo Clinic to Cleveland Clinic. As great as western medicine is, and there was a lot they could rule out, they could never tell us what truly was going in on inside her body.

Michelle also faced the collapse of the mortgage industry. She was one of the top account executives for wholesale lending in the United States, but their world changed literally within days of seeing her company headlining every single news channel out there. One day everyone was thriving; the next, investors were pulling out and the company's stock price was plummeting. Michelle was 39 weeks pregnant with their second daughter Elise and was 100% commission. She never planned to take maternity leave pay because she's always been a non-stop worker (she was closing loans in the hospital bed with their first daughter), but if the company closed, which was the writing on the wall, that meant no income, no insurance. NOTHING! So her doctor said after her 39-week appointment—the same day the stock was plummeting, "I saw your company on the news. It doesn't look good! Do you want to have a baby today? The baby is ready and it's safe." If Michelle did, she would get maternity leave pay for 3 months if her company went under. If she didn't and the company went under, she'd get nothing. So labor was induced and baby Elise was born quickly—just hours later. Two days later Michelle's company was done. Gone. Something she thought she would do forever.

Shawn was also going through huge struggles as well. The higher he climbed the corporate ladder the more time they expected him to be away from his family. In fact, Shawn missed almost all of the first 6 months of his youngest daughter's life while flying back and forth from New York to South Dakota. Because major positions in the bank no longer needed to be based in New York, Shawn's job was to learn the processes involved in daily cash movement of $4 billion up to $40 billion dollars a day, train people back in South Dakota, and fire the people who had been with the bank over 30 years in New York. He was living out of a hotel room in Manhattan Monday through Friday and trying to get home from New York to South Dakota on Friday night, just to be home for less than 48 hours. If one thing went wrong, like sitting on the jetway for an hour or two waiting to take off in typical LaGuardia Friday afternoon fashion, Shawn would miss his connection and not make it home until Saturday, if at all. It was a dog-eat-dog corporate environment that was slowly crushing his soul. At times, the negativity he experienced in the workplace was unfortunately being brought home with him as well. Shawn wasn't the husband, father, or friend he wanted to be. He knew he could be happier! He knew he could be a better man!

Shawn will never forget one weekend he did make it home and was getting ready to leave from the lake they were at for the weekend. His 3-year-old-pulled on his shorts as he was getting ready to leave town again. She looked up at him with her big, round eyes filled with sadness, but hope, and said, "Dad, don't go back." It broke his heart! At that point, he didn't have a choice to not go. How do you try to explain that to a 3-year-old? More importantly, how do you get out of that environment?

They had always been entrepreneurial and owned several of their own businesses, even while doing the corporate trade of time for money, often finding that owning their own businesses was better, but they were their own best employees. Good help is hard to find, and great help is even tougher. They worked nights, weekends, and vacations on their online business. It was a blast and probably kept them afloat during the lean years they faced from 2007-2011, but it wasn't total income replacing type money.

Shawn and Michelle had decisions to make. Although skeptical about entering this profession, they were open minded enough to truly see where it fit in with their lives. You may not be able to change the past, but if you focus on what you're doing in the present, you absolutely can change your future.

Shawn and Michelle had never done anything like this before. They had no experience in the network marketing profession, let alone expertise in the products the company represented. What they did know was this: in business, if others have already shown something to work, they could follow the same system or process and generate similar results. This profession truly can be the great equalizer. It doesn't require any certain education level; your age doesn't matter; and it doesn't look to past experience to determine if you're a fit. It does require a burning desire matched with ambition, coach-ability, and good work ethic.

Shawn and Michelle take anything attached to their name very seriously. It can take years, even decades, to build your name. One wrong decision or move can instantly destroy your name. With skeptical eyes and minds, Michelle tried to disprove the products while Shawn tried to disprove the business model. They couldn't. There was great need in the world for both. They saw this as a mission, a huge, purposeful gift everyone needed, something they quickly became passionate about and allowed them both a full-time profession within 9 months.

The world has never been more connected than it currently is. It's not a matter of if social media platforms are going to change the world and how we operate within it; that's already happened. It's a matter of if you're willing to change how you operate within the new world of social media. Ten years from now the large players within social media may not be Facebook and Instagram, but the world will certainly still operate within some sort of social media playground, and the basic principles of doing business in this environment will not go away.

The world has always placed high importance on providing added value to other people. How can you create content that adds value to not only your current network but also have such value-filled content that it will attract and expand your network indefinitely? Your business will be a direct reflection of the value you add to others through either a product or service. It can be financial impacts, but it will definitely reflect the overall development of people you meet through this profession.

It's always important to have a proper mindset and expectations when you're heading into any new path. The social media world is no exception. Do not over estimate the network you're going to build in the short term because consistency and true added value in the long term will definitely generate such an immense group of people you couldn't possibly run out of people to talk to.

Take the time today to write down your goals on social media. What do you want represented from your social media accounts and the people you ideally want to attract with the content you're providing? Having a strong and clearly written and organized path to build from will streamline your ability to create content that's attracting the right people for you. Without this, you won't be able to assess before you post something whether your content is in alignment with what you want to represent. Never . . . never . . . post something that isn't 100% your true authentic self. You are enough. You are you. People will be drawn to the true you. Have fun!

Questions to ask yourself about your ideal customer or business partner are:

- Age

- Income Level

- Gender

- Hobbies

- Likes and Dislikes

- Specific Regions

- Specific Countries

- Current Buying Patterns

- Education Level

* Get as specific as possible in these questions and note this does not have to be the complete list. Add or subtract information that works best for who you're looking for.

As you create new content for your ideal customer or business partner, quickly check to ensure the post is in alignment with who you're trying to speak to. If it's not, it's probably not something you want posted and attached to your platforms. For example, if your ideal avatar is very health conscious and into clean living and eating, you probably should avoid a picture of the 8-pound plate of nachos cooked up as a snack at midnight. As we tell our children, as soon as you click send, it's out there for the world to see regardless of whether you want it to be or not. Imagine it just got plastered everywhere. If it was sent to one person, assume it could be broadcast and shown to everyone even if you delete it down the road. Another example: if your intent is to avoid polarizing topics but you find yourself writing something that has you on edge about current societal events, is it the right thing to have posted for you? Some people want their identity to be attached to very specific polarizing thoughts and viewpoints. There isn't a wrong or right way to go about this; however, when you create content that is polarizing to one extreme or another, you will alienate and potentially lose a portion of your network. Treat this as your own TV station that is continually putting out content with an intended purpose for a specific audience. You can't be every channel out there trying to broadcast every imaginable desired content worthy of consumption. You won't see a cooking channel trying to also be a sports channel on your TV. Be specific and purposeful!

At first, checking to see if your messaging is in alignment with who you're wanting to attract may seem challenging or unnecessary. Start by printing off your avatar list and carry it with you all day to cross-check. Create content, but BEFORE you post, go through each item on your list and ask if it would resonate with this ideal person. You want each characteristic of your avatar to like, or better yet love, what you're broadcasting. Again, you're like your very own TV channel. What should and shouldn't be on your channel? Like anything else, if done enough, it will become an automatic check you do subconsciously as you go about your day. That's the zone you want to get to!

Social media is allowing us to make meaningful connections from all over the world! What a gift! In network marketing, we are connectors. We are relationship builders! We are collectors of beautiful people! We are here to serve the person in front of us. When you are in the mode of giving instead of receiving, you will grow so much faster. Comment on people's posts! Add value to their posts! Don't just like them. Send them a message and say "loved your post!"

Hop into and join groups that interest you! If you love photography, join photography groups and have fun in them! Add value! Answer questions! Friend others in the group and compliment them! They'll eventually see you on your profile page outside the group, but when you're in the group, you're in the mode to serve them and many others! A relationship is built. Trust is built. They want to get to know you more! Do not spam them! Do not write about your company in the groups. Be a light! It will come back to you. It's so much fun when you can help others. The world needs more of that. Have you heard "The Secret to Living is Giving"? It's true. You will make so many new friends, which will lead to many new business partners or customers. Have fun and be consistent.

Adaptability for change is crucial in the current landscape. The world has never changed more quickly than it currently is. What used to take years or decades to happen in the business environment and social structure we live in can now happen almost overnight. Take into consideration how long some of the social media platforms have been in existence. Facebook started in 2004, Twitter 2006, Instagram 2010, and TikTok 2016—not long at all! As new platforms come out, be adaptable and ahead of the curve in integrating them into your business.

Above all else, whether building person-to-person or online with the various social media platforms, be authentically you. Be passionate, be vulnerable, be true to you. The Poes have found that when they have the most success they are heart driven and truly have the people in front of them in mind as they share and educate on the beauty this profession holds. Raise your standards and change your LIFE! SERVE! LOVE!! Cheer everyone on in this profession.

Be a light. Social Media can be one of the greatest gifts to this planet as long as we do it right—and that's by being a light. Decide to be the light. Decide to serve more and give more than anyone else. Decide to be professional. You are a difference maker! You are a miracle. Have fun making a difference!! Change the world!

MOMENTUM MAKERS

1. **BE AUTHENTICALLY YOU!** Don't try to be someone else. You are good enough. Polish your strengths, sharpen your weaknesses, and continue self development, BUT ALWAYS REMAIN TRUE TO YOURSELF.

2. **LOOK FOR GOLDEN THREADS!** You'll see many recurring patterns of success throughout this book. Take careful note of ideas and concepts that repeat themselves from person to person in these chapters. These are clues to what is proven to work and GOLD for you to put in place for building your empire.

3. **GIVE YOURSELF GRACE!** Chances are you'll be bad before you're good and good before you're great. It's a process of mastery through consistency and reevaluation. Don't overestimate what will be built in the short term, but realize you're probably underestimating what will be built over the next 5-10 years if you do it right.

4. **DO ONE MORE!** Set your goals, and as you accomplish them, do one more. One more meeting. One more presentation. One more follow-up. You'll never run out of actions to build your business by doing one more.

5. **ADAPT TO CHANGE!** If you can master the ability to continually adapt to change and embrace it, you'll be light years ahead of the average person. Social media isn't going away. Look to see where it's heading and get ahead of the curve.

JESSICA MENARD

ZOMBIE MOMMY TO STAY-AT-HOME MOM ENTREPRENEUR

It's 2 a.m. on a Tuesday night, and my phone rings for the 8th time since midnight. The emergency room is on the other end. "A 27-year-old male has been involved in a motor vehicle collision and has just landed via helicopter. He has a traumatic brain injury and needs Neurosurgery to see him immediately." I jump out of my very uncomfortable call bed, put on my shoes, and head downstairs to the ER to see the patient. I AM EXHAUSTED! I haven't seen my kids since I kissed them goodbye yesterday morning while they were still sleeping. This day on call seems to never end. I keep asking myself, "Do I love being a neurosurgical physician assistant (PA)?" YES! "Do I love helping others?" YES! "Do I work for incredible doctors and have amazing coworkers?" YES!

But my mind wanders back to my sleeping babies. I am missing so much: taking my kids to school, Lilly's ballet practice, Wesley's karate meet, moments that I prayed so hard to have. My babies just turned 5, and unfortunately, my family's nickname for me is "Zombie Mommy." Pretty sad right? I am so exhausted after each 24+ hour shift, so it's no surprise that I bear some resemblance to a zombie. All I can do is crash into my bed, get some rest, and get ready to do it all over again. Time is flying by, my children are growing up, and I am missing out. I tell myself, "Something has to change."

Fast-forward a couple months to October 2013. Our pastor is speaking about how God cares about the little things and we should take all of our cares, frustrations, and worries to Him in prayer, no matter how big or small. My husband and I are blessed with good jobs, a wonderful home, and healthy children. How can I possibly complain? After that sermon, though, I realized my desire to be home was BIG to me. My husband and I immediately prayed for a way for me to be home, to be more present as a mother and a wife. I was so tired of being "Zombie Mommy" and most of all feeling like it.

Just a few days later, I get a message from a PA classmate, Stephanie Young, asking if she could share an opportunity with me. Cue the eye roll! I wondered what she's going to try to sell me, but I was curious. She's a PA like me. Why is she doing something else, and what is it? I agreed to hop on a call with her. What would it hurt? I remember her being such a nice person in school, and we hadn't caught up in years. I decide to chat, be kind, and politely say "no" to whatever she was selling.

The next day she called, and I reluctantly answered. She shared what she was doing in the skincare industry, and I listened . . . well, somewhat. I was too busy thinking how I would let her down politely. I said, "Thank you so much for thinking of me, but I am WAY too busy, and I am not a salesperson. However, I'd love to try your skincare." With 5-year-old twins and tons of trauma calls, I obviously needed help with my skin and the bags under my eyes. I would try anything to combat that zombie mommy look! I quickly fell in love with the products, and when coworkers asked me if I "changed makeup," I found myself sharing all the awesome products I started using. All I can say is "hallelujah for some incredible eye cream!" Who loves their dark circles anyway? Not me. I continued to share, but at the same time I kept telling myself that network marketing was not for me. Funny, right? What would people think? I am not being conned into some "pyramid scheme." Well, well, well, I could not have been more wrong.

Over the next few months, I watched Stephanie grow her business while working as a pediatric PA and mom to two toddlers. She followed up with me and shared what the business was doing for her family, but I stubbornly continued to dismiss it. On Valentine's Day, 2014, she shared that she was retiring as a PA thanks to her business; that's when I second-guessed my previous dismissal! "What? No way!" I could NOT have heard that message correctly. I replayed and replayed it. I was sitting in the car with my husband on the way back from dinner, and my mind was spinning. I told him what Stephanie shared and finally said, "I am calling her tomorrow!" I made the call, but this time, things were very different.

I listened. I really listened; there was no eye-rolling on this call. I finally HEARD what she was sharing—the opportunity to market a #1 brand to people with skin. HELLO! It clicked! Was this the opportunity I prayed for?

On February 15, 2014, I became an independent consultant for my brand. I was in business and decided that although I didn't have time and wasn't a salesperson, I was going to give it 100% by being coachable and consistent and working my business in some little way every day. I was so green and definitely had a lot to learn, but I knew from listening to leaders that I didn't have to know everything overnight before getting started. I just had to start.

I committed to learn something new about my business every day and decided to watch a training video each week. I was a CEO, right? I needed to act like it, even though I was a team of one. I was also taught the importance of personal development, so I decided to fill my brain and soul with a few pages of something positive every day. Stephanie shared that this type of business is not a get-quick-rich scheme but a legitimate business that would take time to grow. Got it! Crockpot, not microwave! The more I read on network marketing and residual income, the more I wanted to kick myself for not jumping in months ago. Why didn't I listen? Why was I so opposed to an opportunity outside of the traditional 9-5 (or in my case 7 a.m. to 7 a.m.)? Why didn't Stephanie beat me over the head until I listened? Well, you know the phrase about spilled milk right? I was frustrated with myself, but it was time to get started.

I wanted to share with you all of the feelings, thoughts, and eye rolls I had prior to joining my company because I think these types of responses are so common. Most people have never been taught about residual income. Most people don't understand the concept of network marketing and associate those two words with two other dirty words: PYRAMID SCHEME. The idea of making money while you sleep is totally foreign. We think a traditional job for 40+ hours a week for 40 years is the only way to truly be successful. We trade time and moments to get ahead in our jobs, which in so many cases rob us of the moments that we can never get back. I get all of that because I was that person. I didn't realize that while I was a customer and sharing products that I loved, I was already in network marketing. I just wasn't getting anything in return other than a happy friend. We share products we love all the time. Our friends and family (our networks) hear our enthusiasm and go out and try that very product, restaurant, or pair of shoes. I don't feel like I am selling something to them. I genuinely love the product and genuinely want them to try it. Network marketing is no different. They fall in love and start to share with their networks and so on and so on. It is as simple as that. It's not brain surgery. The minute we make it icky, weird, or fake, it feels icky, weird, and fake to the person to whom we are talking.

I thought about all of this when I started my business. How did I want to present myself as a new business owner? How did I want to share the products? I had built a solid reputation in so many arenas, and I didn't want to jeopardize that in any way. But I felt clueless. How do I start? What do I say? So I came up with a brilliant idea: I decided to be me, just me. I decided to confidently put myself out there. The products were #1, the research and clinical studies were on point, the founders had an impeccable reputation and years of experience, and most of all, the products worked. Nothing was on trial there! Even though I was just starting this new chapter,

I wanted my friends and family to see what I didn't see for months—the importance of a Plan B and how that Plan B can become Plan A. I wanted them to see that there is another way, and although that way may be foreign to them, network marketing and social commerce are legitimate and real ways to have the financial and time freedom we all crave. If they couldn't see it immediately, I just had to do what Stephanie did: be the example and prove it!

When I first launched my business, I focused on being authentic. I wanted to convey that I used the products, loved the results, and decided to share them in hopes of giving others the opportunity to get the same results. Looking back, I will admit now, my first few posts were pretty bad . . . really bad. I wasn't social media savvy. My pictures didn't crop correctly. My verbiage was too much. I beat myself up for not having Instagram-worthy photos with the perfect preset on lighting. However, I was enthusiastic, so I had that going for me. I posted consistently, not too little and not too much. Social media was such an asset in the beginning and throughout my entire journey because it allowed me to convey what I was doing to a large group of people, which sparked numerous conversations. However, social media DOES NOT, I repeat DOES NOT, replace a phone call, coffee date, or business presentation. I made sure to follow up on every conversation with a scheduled call, coffee date, or invite to an event.

Since I started, I have watched over the years as people join companies, completely hide behind social media, and wonder why their businesses aren't growing. They get frustrated and do one of two things wrong. They either start posting more about their business, essentially annoying their network with 5-6 posts a day, or they stop talking about their businesses all together. Wrong and wrong. I decided that my life is made up of so many different chapters coming together in one beautiful story. This adventure would be just one of those chapters. I took turns highlighting each facet of my life: my family, my faith, my hobbies, my travel adventures, and my excitement about my business and products. I shared before and after photos and stuck to the facts of my business. I made sure my pictures were actual portrayals of results and my verbiage was on point. I still made a few mistakes on occasion, but the beauty of social media is you can go back and correct and improve. I did this EVERY SINGLE DAY without fail. My network's curiosity began to take over. Why is this Neurosurgical Physician Assistant selling skincare? Why did she choose this? What is this company? It's so funny because these were the same questions I had in my mind when Stephanie was messaging me.

People started asking more questions, showing up to presentations, and hopping on calls with Stephanie and me. I certainly didn't know it all at this early point or how to deal with objections, so that's why the help of a leader or sponsor is so essential. If you're new, don't try to pretend. I was just honest and authentic, and my friends appreciated that. Stephanie was able to answer all of their questions, and I learned how to duplicate this process. I became more confident in my presentations and the ability to share the information without vomiting the facts all over anyone who expressed any interest. The more events I hosted, calls and coffee dates I scheduled, and the more interest I got, the more my business began to take off. Did everyone say "yes"? Absolutely not! Did people ignore my messages about the opportunity? ALL THE TIME!

Let me stop right here and elaborate a little more on dealing with those "No's" and having belief in your journey. I learned very early on that it's a numbers game. I heard that time and time again in trainings after I started my business, but I didn't really believe it. I already had so many people signed up in my head for products or for becoming my business partner. At first, when they said "no" or completely ignored me, it hurt. My very first negative response on social media was actually from a lifelong friend. Thirty seconds after I posted that I had joined my new company, I was immediately messaged asking if I had been scammed. She went on to say how she couldn't believe I would join a pyramid scheme and asked if I really thought I was going to make money. The comments hurt my heart.

I had so much belief in the products, the business, and my own personal results. She was the very person that had already partnered with me in my head. I could have allowed that to completely derail me, but something inside urged me to hold my chin up and move on.

Early on, I quickly realized, it is a numbers game. Not everyone will get what you are doing and why you're doing it. We can either let it completely divert our paths and possibly steal the opportunities and blessings ahead, or we can continue to positively represent the brand in hopes that they will see it for themselves. Over the years, so many of my original "NO's" have turned into "YES's!" It all boils down to your belief and your numbers. If you are starting a business, you have to truly believe in what you are selling and the channel in which you are selling it. They say belief has a sound, and that is absolutely true. If you are not confident in your products or channel, people will immediately be able to sense it, and that's a turn off. Be authentic! Be yourself! Share why you love what you do and why you are doing it. Even if you are not perfectly polished, people will trust you because of your authenticity, belief, and excitement, and they will want to know more. I love the quote by Dr. Ivan Misner, "Ignorance on fire is better than knowledge on ice." Don't let anyone steal your fire. If you are not sure of your why, take the time to peel back the onion to figure it out, then put yourself out there.

Marketing a business demands consistency. When I started, I agreed to be consistent. I was told that it takes 3 months of daily, consistent activity before you start to see the fruits of your labor. Most people are watching you from day one. Most don't respond because they are either busy or, maybe, they're just waiting to see if you will be consistent. Do her products really work? Will she be successful in this business? If you only post once every other week, people can certainly see that you are not enthusiastic about your new endeavor. No one will be interested in something if you are not. Lack of consistency may also convey a lack of knowledge, and they may assume you don't know enough about what you are selling. I have had numerous people over the years reach out to purchase products from me or join the company because they saw that over time I was consistent about sharing the products and business.

This process went on day after day. Posting on social media, three-way calls with my sponsor, duplicating three-way calls with my team, scheduling events, and following up with those interested. All of my efforts and late nights started to pay off. Within my first month, I had earned enough to pay off my investment into the business, which included our largest assortment of regimens and products. By my third month, I was at the top 2% of the company and went on to earn an awesome trip to Napa. By 12 months, we were a car-achieving team, which essentially meant we had seven-figure annual sales. Plus, I earned a trip to Maui. By 14 months, I was earning more monthly than my PA position. Just shy of 2 years, I left my full-time PA job and traded my "Zombie Mommy" name tag for the title of stay-at-home mom entrepreneur!

I cannot even begin to describe the feelings I felt on that first day in January 2016. The feelings were all over the place. It would go from praising GOD, then to shock, then tears, and then I'd repeat it all over again. I could FINALLY be in the moment instead of in a cloud of fatigue and caffeine. Did I quit my job all together? NO! I worked hard to earn that degree, the reputation, the skills, and the friendships. I go in to help in the operating room or see patients once a week or once every other week. The difference is now it's on my time and only if it works for my schedule. And guess what? I am such a better PA. I enjoy the moments more and love helping patients on the path to recovery. I go in and work a few hours and leave just in time to grab my kiddos in carpool! YESSSSS!! Time freedom is priceless.

There are so many things that I wanted to convey to you in this chapter from my story. First of all, believe in yourself. You can do this! Dig deeply into why you are doing your business. Hold that close to your heart and get laser focused. So often in life we allow others' opinions to dictate what we can and cannot do. Push those opinions aside because as Deepak Chopra said, "What other people think of you is none of your business."

Focus on your goals, grasp your belief, and make the decision to just do it. Don't miss one more moment. Don't wait until you know everything to get started in your business. None of us is perfect, and we are growing and learning every day. It's your enthusiasm and authenticity that will attract the people that you will enjoy working with anyway. Be ready to do the work! Social media is an incredible assistant on your journey, but YOU have to put yourself out there on a daily basis. You have to be willing to make the phone call, schedule the coffee date, and plan the event. You have to be willing to do it over and over again, no matter the outcome.

Be a CEO from day one and decide to be the leader you want to follow, even when you are the only one on your team. The "NO's" will come, and sometimes they will be from someone you love and respect. Just be kind, remember why YOU are doing this, and keep pressing forward. They might surprise you in the future.

Finally, enjoy the journey! Celebrate every win no matter how big or small and duplicate that in your team. This business is something different, so make it that way. People are looking for different; they are looking for something exciting and positive, so mold your team into a culture that everyone wants to be a part of.

I am so thankful to be a part of this incredible book with Jordan Adler and so many other amazing men and women. I am thankful that GOD placed me on a path that I never thought I would walk. I am thankful for each and every customer who believed in me and our products and for each team member who brings something unique and incredible to the table. I am truly humbled to be where I am at this very moment and thrilled to see what GOD has planned in the future. My why is to walk out my calling in this thing called life and enjoy every moment. GOD BLESS!

MOMENTUM MAKERS

1. **BE YOU . . . AUTHENTICALLY YOU!!!** People in your network trust you. You don't have to be the perfectly polished social media guru with perfect light settings to get started. Share why you love what you do, and why you are doing it. People will trust you because of your authenticity, belief, and excitement. This authenticity will spark conversations. You don't want to look or sound like anyone but YOU!

2. **"BRANDING" SOUNDS COMPLICATED! NO!** It's the easiest thing to do. Pick 4-5 things that you love and set up a schedule to highlight those things on social media. In addition to those, highlight your business each day so that it's not missed. Mine are family, travel, Christianity, farming, my skincare business . . . and maybe coffee.

3. **CONSISTENCY IS KEY!** No one will be interested in something if you are not. Sometimes your network is watching to see if you are consistent in your excitement about your product and business. Now, excitement doesn't mean posting 5-6 times a day. That's a big NO! However, lack of consistency may also convey a lack of knowledge to your network. People want to buy from or join someone that they feel confident knows the product line or someone that can coach them to success.

4. **IT'S ALL ABOUT RELATIONSHIPS.** Social media does not replace a genuine relationship! Get to know the person first, no matter the outcome. PEOPLE FIRST! Become a friend and just be authentic. Don't hide behind social media posts and wonder

MOMENTUM MAKERS

why your business isn't growing. Schedule the coffee date or phone call. Focus on what their needs are versus yours!

5. **DON'T BE AFRAID OF CHANGE:** Social media is changing all the time! IG and FB Stories, going LIVE, posting do's and don'ts, commenting, filters . . . the list goes on and on. Don't let this slow your roll. Now, I am not saying to get stuck in the dark ages of My Space. Just take the time to learn a little more each week and perfect your art and keep sharing. Jump out there each day with enthusiasm.

JODY CHASE

FROM MBA... TO CEO OF BUILDING A BETTER WAY

If somebody told me that I'd become a millionaire (and then some) through network marketing, I'd have first laughed and then googled "network marketing" to see what that meant. Growing up in an affluent New England town, my parents had instilled in me from an early age to "study hard, get good grades and a good degree (or 2 or 3), and you can get a great job and live happily ever after." So I literally did, and in the process, I realized, that path and system is absolutely broken (for women in particular). I'm super grateful for network marketing as it has allowed me to create a life, a living, and a legacy while building a platform to help others win, not just me, and I say that as somebody who never really thought she was going to be able to make such a difference in the world.

I wasn't ever the popular girl, the smart girl, or the "great at sports" girl in school, and I never knew exactly "what I wanted to be when I grew up," so I followed the trail that others had blazed before me. I wasn't a "leader" back then; I was very much a rule-follower and landed in civil engineering. (Let's be honest, the male/female ratio there was super favorable, and while many of my sorority sisters struggled to land great jobs after graduation, I had my pick of several great offers.) It was not the easiest major, but I liked a good challenge and loved that it was practical and was a combination of numbers, facts, and know-how. It also uses creative and analytical thinking—so, life seemed "on track."

My first brush with entrepreneurship came from working with the land developers for whom I designed projects and roadways. As I helped them design and build, I started to see bigger opportunities, and I wanted more. Why wasn't I on other side of the table, building something, designing a vision, bringing it to life, and getting paid well to do it? I figured getting another degree would give me the clarity and skills I needed to figure out my next move, right? In true rule-following fashion, I spent the next few years earning my MBA at the Sloan School at MIT. I have no idea how I got accepted, to be honest, but I remember telling my interviewer, "Coach, put me in the game. I'm not super fancy, I don't have a pedigree or legacy family as benefactors, and I didn't go to an ivy undergrad, but I'm meant to do big things, and I need a way to find my voice and I need to play on a different field to do it."

Only $120K in student loans later, my biggest lessons didn't revolve around finance skills (I got those, too, of course); they came from looking to my left and right in those lecture halls, sitting among the most brilliant people in the world every single day, and realizing that most of them didn't have it figured out for themselves either. I was just as smart, just as capable, and had access to all the same resources they did. But I continued into a corporate finance position after business school because that that was the expected next step.

After grinding away for 6+ years in finance, I saw themes emerge. The upper leadership at my company spent more time with pictures of their children than they did with their children themselves, and there was no exit plan, no end game. I'd "made it," right? I had a high-paying career in finance with lots of options to keep advancing but at what cost? I didn't see a way to make a living and also have a life. My life looked shiny and attractive from the outside, but inside it was soul-crushing. My husband and I could barely take care of a puppy; how on earth were we going to start a family? Academically, I knew all about leverage and about residual income, but I'd painted myself into a corner and into a career that had no leverage, no time, no life, and no future plan that I really could get excited about. I had come to terms with the fact that I'd always have to work hard and not have time or financial freedom. But my mind knew better, and I began searching for a better way, although it was only subconsciously at the beginning.

When our first child was born, I left finance entirely and fell into a new mom identity crisis; we fell into a financial crisis, too. Since I'd only been making the interest payments on my student loans, I still had $109K in debt, and we'd just bought a new home in a brand new town where I knew nobody. My husband came home from work one day to find me bawling on the bottom step of our staircase. What had I done? I had debt, uncertainty, no friends locally, and the onslaught of postpartum hormones, all of which were the recipe for a perfect storm.

I became an expert coupon clipper for the next few years, and we lived month-to-month treading water, judiciously accounting for every penny and hoping for a better way, so that I didn't have to return to a corporate career. Truth be told, I even used my Top 3 Business School skills to leverage $300K in credit card debt, parked in various bank accounts to earn 6% interest—talk about being entrepreneurial. Where was network marketing during those first few years?

I crossed paths with network marketing by accident. We'd just had our second child and moved to another new town (again, where I knew nobody), and a friend encouraged me to take a look at some baby products that her company offered. We'd always lived a pretty healthy lifestyle, using products that had "natural" labels, and I thought that if my products said "organic" or "non-toxic" I was doing an extra great job, right? Well, I started to realize that just about every personal care and home cleaning product in my home at the time contained harmful ingredients. I started to connect the dots; that's why I had eczema on my eyelids and rashes on my arms, and that's why I got a migraine every time I cleaned the house.

My friend showed me the results that others were having, and without having ever been to an event or trying the products myself, I signed myself up as a consultant to get the personal discount. I was a smart person, right? A discount was way better than full-price. She showed me how to order and how to share with others if I chose. Wait, what? I could earn money by sharing? Was this a thing? Could I build a business? After a short course on the compensation plan during a 2 a.m. baby feeding, I had absolutely no idea how I was going to do this, but I was going to do it. My thought at the time was that I knew the products were game-changing and would help people live better and have total peace-of-mind, and I didn't have to sell my soul or lose my friends to share them. I was all in. This was the way I could afford karate studio fees, soccer, organic groceries, and car payments.

Having zero experience was both a blessing and a curse, but above all, it is proof positive that network marketing is a far better way for someone with ambition yet without capital and resources to build an empire and have a positive impact on themselves, their family, and the world. Over the last 7 years I've built my organization in one single company. I paid off that remaining $109K in student loan debt in my first 18 months. I've built residual (happens more than once) and leveraged (happens based upon the efforts of others) income that can grow without my direct effort. I've seen parts of my organization fall apart. I've seen thousands of people join and thousands of people quit, and I've seen countless new leaders rise up and change their lives, and we're just getting started. The fact that success is a possibility for other people is just ridiculously incredible. Grateful is not a big enough word to describe how I feel about what network marketing has given me and I've never had to be somebody that I'm not, or join the "NFL" (No Friends Left club) to do it, I saw the opportunity and made the choice.

Below are my top tips for building a life and a lifestyle that you love through network marketing.

1. All business is conversation. Whether you start conversations through social media or in real life, the quality of your conversations and your ability to connect with people on a human level is what will make them open to learning more about what you can offer them. That's why posting your replicated links on social media does more harm than good and why networking in real life will never get old. Do you care about them or are you just trying to sell something? Be honest with people; if you're new and nervous, tell them. If you think your product can help them, tell them why. Whether they're open or not is their decision, but it's our job to start the conversation.

2. Be a consultant, not a salesperson. The number one fear I hear new team members articulate is that they don't want to be "salesy" or "pushy." No one wants to see a social feed full of advertisements. Here's a new perspective: salespeople tend to have the transaction and the benefit to themselves in mind (self-focused) whereas consultants focus on helping the person they're talking with arrive at a decision that makes most sense for them (others-focused). Consultants ask questions and make recommendations to help people. Focus on who you can help and how and you will never feel "salesy." When posting on social, ask your audience questions that will provide insights into their lives and needs/wants. The conversations about what you can offer them will take care of themselves as people follow you and you become a trusted voice.

3. Everybody matters, but invest your time where it's deserved, not where it's needed. Most people don't set out to earn 6/7-figures annually, so that's not ever the vision I lead with. As a mom who was clipping coupons and driving from store to store to generate more coupons, an extra $300 a month was the difference between me needing to look at going back to work and buying myself some more time to see what I could turn this into. For the average household, $300 a month is the difference between having more "month" than money available and having a little breathing room that can bring them financial peace, and it's a race to get somebody to this level of success, before they let the gravitational forces of life, self-doubt and distractions knock them out! Social media gives you an inside look at where your team is spending their time. Are they absent on social entirely? There's a good chance they're avoiding their business also. Are they posting about their day at the beach? That's an insight as to where their head is also. There are people literally praying for an opportunity like the one that you have, and when you have somebody who is hungry for more and willing to take action, that is where you put your time, regardless of their title. If they've said they want significant success, hold them to it! People will always ask for your time, but prioritize those who are in action.

4. Bloom where you are planted. The longer you are in this profession, the more hype, shiny objects, and plain "B.S." you'll have the opportunity to witness ☺. There's no magic "simple system to get to the top," and you can't go very far if you aren't willing to actually talk with people. Hero products will come and go. There are no "industry disruptors" that last more than a season. If you're stuck, perhaps you may need to reinvent yourself and your attitude where you are. We all get stuck—it's just a matter of when and what you do about it. We all have major ups and downs, and believe me, I know what it feels like to want to quit over and over. But while it may seem like an escape hatch or a "fresh start" to reinvent yourself elsewhere where the grass seems more "green", the reality is that you can reinvent yourself right where you are. It's simply a decision because ultimately, wherever you go, there you are. Success or failure is entirely up to you. Being successful stems from the decision to dig in, and you can do that right where you are if you can get your ego out of the way. The only exception to this, in my opinion, is when your company is out of ethics and/or there's a fundamental issue with the leadership and their strategic direction. Find a company with a message that means something to you with products that you'd buy even if there wasn't a compensation plan attached. Check out the company leadership, find a great team to join that has proven success stories, and go! Tell your story and bring people along on your journey.

5. The size of the challenge that you can successfully navigate, determines the size of your leadership ability. Tough times don't last; tough people do. Weeks after earning my highest check ever in network marketing and living in the sweet spot of full-blown company momentum, the owners of our original company decided to step away from the business without warning. We were told that the company would continue on and eventually be sold, but aside from that, every variable was unknown. I'd enrolled thousands of people by that point. What was I supposed to tell them? Should I wait and see? Should I find a new home where I knew the waters were more calm? Should I put on a brave face and "tell my team whatever necessary to keep them engaged"? We were about a week away from putting our house on the market to move to a bigger one, and poof, everything I'd worked so hard to build over the last 4 years was imploding before my eyes. I'd not planned for anything like this, and naïve as I was in our business model, it honestly hadn't ever occurred to me that this could happen. But it's in the most difficult moments that you'll be tested as a leader. The right move won't always appear obvious. I gave myself 20 minutes to rein in my own hysteria and throw some choice objects across the room, then I got to work. I found out all I could, factually, about the landscape, and I was honest with our team about what I knew, how our company was problem-solving, what we were going to do right now to move ourselves forward, and, at the end of the day, how very grounded we still were in the positive fundamentals of making phenomenal products that people needed and wanted.

As with any "company closure story" the social media drama came fast and furious. False rumors, allegations, and recruiting pitches took over my dms. When there's drama, you'll always see the opportunists flock to capitalize on it—but what comes easily, goes just as easily too. I poured my heart into serving my team, holding frequent calls, sending updates, and over-communicating to combat some of the abandonment that many were feeling. I painted our new vision, built belief, and showcased all the success stories the I could. Together, we navigated a 2-year shift to the culture we are exploding with today. Not all stayed. Not all kept and built their belief. But the ones who have and who have continued to build and re-build are stronger and more resilient leaders as a result. Things don't happen to you; they happen for you. That next big obstacle that's waiting for you may very well be the kick in the pants that you need to become the influential leader that you are meant to be.

6. Be willing to tolerate the mis-educated opinions of others who don't understand our business model. There are three perspectives people tend to have about network marketing: they either love and support it, they're indifferent and don't know about it, or they've had a bad experience and/or embody some type of broken programming. None of these viewpoints have anything to do with you, your product, or your company! Maybe they joined a business once and didn't actually do anything. Maybe they had a poor product experience somewhere. Maybe their friend joined something and sent them spammy Private Messages every day and they're assuming you're going to as well. Either way, their opinion has exactly zero to do with your potential for success, and it's important for you to know that right up front. There will be dream stealers and people who literally don't want you to have success, but you're the brave one! You're the one who said "yes" to an opportunity, and maybe they're not quite brave enough to do that themselves.

7. Your business is a "leaky bucket," and what gets you to a rank/ level won't necessarily keep you there or take you to the next one. We are in the building and re-building business! Algorithms and visibility changes. Customers don't always re-order. Some of them continue re-ordering for months or years, and some will stay for decades. Team members may join for a season of their lives (Holiday spending money? Stuck inside glued to social media with a pandemic going on?), or they may reach a certain level, then lose confidence or have a major life circumstance that pulls them away from daily activity. Think of your business as a leaky bucket; you've got to be adding "water" (new customers and team members) to the bucket faster than the water is escaping through the holes (having customers stop ordering or team members quit, either emotionally or literally). When you hit your first big rank, it's so tempting to assume that your team will continue to grow in the same proportion that it did to get you there. The great news is that there does come a point where duplication happens and new leaders can emerge without you directly creating them.

8. Swim with both arms. Ever tune into a great training and felt like, "Whew! I completely up-leveled my mindset today!" This may be true; however, learning skills and personal development alone won't actually build your business. It's what you do with what you learn that matters! Think of it like swimming; if you only learn, study, and plug into development, you're swimming with one arm and will swim around in circles with no forward progress. But when you combine that with actual business activities that lead to new customers and new team members, now you're covering some distance. Both matter, and you've got to balance them one for one if you want to swim in a straight line.

9. The truth is good enough! Course-correcting an excited new team member isn't my favorite thing, but it's my job to mentally prepare them for the realities of our business. No, you can't just parrot the company messaging. You can't just share posts from others. Our products don't "sell themselves." This isn't "super easy," and not "everyone can do it." When we use these kinds of phrases, we attract people looking to get in, make money, and not work, and as soon as they're met with a challenge or an objection, they won't have the mindset to continue in the business because they were sold the idea that it was going to be easy. Showcase the truth; the truth is beautiful, and it's more than good enough. For the newer team members who want to earn some income, they have to know this is entrepreneurship. Is this business complicated? Not at all. It's simple but not easy. And if the products sold themselves, the company wouldn't need us. There will be ups and downs; there will be people who tell you "no," there will be people who unfollow you and you will want to quit. But there are people who have gone before you and paved a path, and we will show you exactly how to get through all of those times.

10. Use your network marketing business to build true wealth. Cash flow is one thing; building wealth is quite another. It can be thrilling to see your first 3-figure, 4-figure, or 5-figure check, but if you don't develop some financial literacy skills and practices alongside your network marketing income, it's very easy to get stuck still living "paycheck to paycheck" and trying to keep up with a lifestyle that so many of us want to showcase, amIright? We've all seen people who as they earn more spend much more, and it's a fatal error. Money is a fascinating thing, and we all grow up with so many deep-seated thoughts and feelings surrounding money: earning, spending, and/or investing it. And that warrants an entire book in and of itself. On a basic level, look at your network marketing business as a way to generate cash that you can invest (not spend) into other things (financial investments, real estate, etc.) that will generate even more income for your family beyond your own lifetime. That's building wealth. Should you buy a new bag, those Valentinos you've been eyeing, or take a vacation? Absolutely! Treat yourself on occasion if you feel you've earned it, but know that true wealth building isn't so much about the size of your check; it's about what you do with it!

Network marketing introduced me to a phenomenal product that I'd buy even if it didn't have a compensation plan attached to it. It's allowed me to get healthier, live/look and feel better, and create residual and leveraged income to not just help pay our bills and allow me to work from home with my young kids but to build the legacy that I plan to pass forward to future generations. It's the very best kept secret and most brilliant business model in the world, and that's coming from someone versed in the world of business and who has earned high six figures in the traditional business world as well. My only regret is that I didn't get started sooner than I did, and I can promise you that there's absolutely room at the table for you!

—————— MOMENTUM MAKERS ——————

1. **SOCIAL MEDIA IS NOT YOUR BUSINESS, IT'S ONLY A TOOL.** Who you are as a person and your ability to connect and communicate with people is amplified when you add social media into your toolbox – it's a platform though, not a strategy. You've got to get your fundamentals right in real life first – be a person of value to others, be able to start conversations and build relationships, and be the bridge to what you offer, before you'll be able to use social media to reach new people and build a business.

2. **IF YOU'RE THE LEAST BIT BUSINESS-SAVVY OR ENTREPRENEURIAL, NETWORK MARKETING IS A BRILLIANT DECISION!** Where else in the world can you start a real business for less than $500, with the backend structures already in place? Product development, manufacturing, packaging, shipping – done for you. You simply serve as the bridge between what you offer, and the people you can help and build a culture around that through leadership. Coming from the investment and finance world, I know what it takes to build a successful company from the ground up, and most traditional businesses fail because of cash flow – which is a non-issue for us!

3. **WHAT DO YOU *REALLY* WANT?** So many of us follow paths that others have paved and measure our successes in life against yard sticks created by others. Life is now and our time is limited, so don't waste it living someone else's life. Is the path that you're on going to bring you fulfillment, wealth, and freedom down the road? Be brave enough to step out of line and start

something of your own. Don't wait for permission or approval from others, find a product and a mission you believe in and a great mentor who can teach you to do what they've done – and go!

4. **WHOEVER BELIEVES THE MOST, WINS!** When you believe in what you're sharing and how it can help others, people will stop and listen. If you're shaky on what you offer or the value you bring to others, or you're just copying-and-pasting things without any authenticity or connection, they'll ignore you.

5. **BUILD TRUE WEALTH.** Don't increase your lifestyle as you begin to earn extra money. Absolutely, take care of your immediate needs and some deserved non-negotiables (mine are food, wine and having fun), but invest a significant part of your earnings into things that will generate even more income for your family beyond your current lifestyle – think real estate and other financial vehicles. That's how you use your business to leave a legacy!

CHRISTINA WATTS
RELATABLE MARKETING

I was just your average American woman, living the life that society taught her and working that nine-to-five "Corporate America" job. I remember the days when I thought my only option was to go to my first job as a police dispatcher, head from there to my second job as a photographer, then go home to spend just one hour with my son. I knew there had to be more to life than living to work all day and missing out on every family event and every first milestone of my baby's life. However, my skepticism about alternate means of income held me back. It's not uncommon to be skeptical about different opportunities outside of the "norm"; most people are skeptical about these types of opportunities.

However, despite my skepticism, at the age of 24 I decided that my life needed to go a down a different path, including my limited mindset about the options I truly had. I was mentally done spending my days in a negative environment only to get one hour out of the day with my son.

I decided to make a life change! I dove head first into network marketing and jumped with two feet into the opportunity I was presented with at that time. I didn't let ANYTHING stop me. In my mind, I had no other choice but to give it my all, especially if I wanted to get out of my current situation. I made the decision that it didn't matter what anyone else said about the new journey I was on. I was going to make it work. I would be successful, and I would never look back! I remember my co-workers making bets on how long it would be until I gave up; they said I would fail. That just ignited my fire.

My WHY was so huge—I needed a job that would empower, not limit, time with my son; but I didn't know at first how I was going to make it work! I was working two full-time jobs on top of being a busy mom, but my son was my why, and I was going to do everything in my power to change my life for him! I put my head into the game, ran full force, and learned everything about the company I was a part of and exactly what I had in my hands! I continuously told myself that my only option was to succeed!

When I started network marketing, I didn't have a single clue what I was doing. It was no different from when I got hired as a dispatcher, though. I didn't have a single clue what that job REALLY entailed, either. How was I going to learn everything I needed to in order to be a good dispatcher? But, I did learn everything I needed to and was good at what I did. The same is true of network marketing!

I think the biggest struggle for people that jump into network marketing is that they honestly don't treat it like a job. People don't always understand when they get started that they have to learn everything about the business that they are a part of, just like they would at any job in corporate America. When I saw others succeeding on this journey and making it a full-time career, I knew I could make a career out of it as well.

Within 5 months of joining my company, I was able to quit both of my jobs and become a work-from-home mom. Can you imagine the feeling I had when I got to turn in my 2-week notice? I was finally able to breathe. I was going to get to raise my baby and never miss a moment! I could pay our bills and still have enough money to buy things that weren't necessities. I could give back to my family, friends, and complete strangers without having to worry if my bank account was going to be in the red zone. Most do not know the struggles I went through and call me lucky. I was lucky enough to be able to do this in their eyes, but this was not easy, and it was not luck. I treated this opportunity like a third full-time job and worked at it every possible chance I had.

I started in this business and built it from the ground up with only 160 friends on social media. At first, I didn't even really know how to navigate any social media platform. Once I did some more research, I found out that there were over a billion people on social media daily! That's crazy! I knew I was going to utilize this tool because of the amazing opportunity for growth and because it was free. I got over my fear of letting strangers view my pages. I told my husband, who was a police officer at the time, that I was just going to make sure that I didn't post anything that I didn't want the world to see. Social media really is a way to make a lot of money in a short time as long as you open up and allow as many people as possible access your pages. From the day I started until now, six years later, I have reached over 200,000 people on my social media accounts.

While passionately pursuing my dreams with this opportunity daily, I have really focused on what I refer to as "relatable marketing." What is relatable marketing? Let me explain. When people log into Facebook, they are there to see reality, the real lives of those they are connected to. They want to see things that they can relate to on social media, people and things they can make a connection with on a daily basis. Maybe it's that tired mom who happens to see another post from a tired, busy mom with whom she can totally relate! Maybe it's a lady looking for a recipe, and she just happens to see your post of an easy recipe, and boom, she wants to make that for dinner. When someone goes on Facebook, they don't typically go on there to shop. Your goal is to get people to fall in love with you before they can fall in love with anything you have to offer. For me personally, it's busy moms with chaotic lives because I can totally relate to them!

Bringing people to your page and KEEPING them on your page is KEY! I have never gone to Facebook, saw someone post every product in their catalog and thought, "Wow, I should buy from them!" I just haven't.

However, I have gone to Facebook and loved and enjoyed following certain people. Conversely, when I have been following them, totally love what I see, and have already built a social media relationship with them, I'm immediately interested in whatever it is they have to offer whenever they promote a product or company. I have built trust with them, even though it's through social media. You trust the person that you love to follow, so you trust what they are promoting.

I never wanted to spam and nag my friends and family with a business opportunity or products. I wanted to grow my network so large that I wouldn't have to reach out to people so much. Instead I wanted them to reach out to me, and eventually, they did. I keep everything very vague on my pages; my goal is to build their curiosity. I want people to be able to build that relationship with me. I want them to feel comfortable asking me questions. I also want them to trust me when I give them the information, rather than just googling what I have to offer because they saw it on my page (say a post I made about that exact product or a before and after picture). If that person then finds one bad review, they are likely to never have that conversation with me. This is why I use relatable posts and curiosity posts and steer away from any catalog posting.

Be yourself on Facebook. Be real and genuine. People will relate to you no matter the type of person you are. Find your relatable audience. The most-watched television show genre is reality TV. Now that you can go live on social media, that's about as real as it gets. Interact with your audience and the new faces on your social media by going live! Going "Live" is like you are on FaceTime or Zoom with them, but instead of talking, you are engaging with them through the comments. Once you stop trying to be like someone you aren't and you are just yourself, you will start to find that more people will hop on your videos or even comment on your posts.

When you post relatable things that people can see themselves doing, they will be attracted to your page. My ultimate goal is for every single one of my friends and followers to come to my page every morning just to see what has been posted. Just like people binge-watch reality TV, I want them to binge-watch my page.

When I train others on relatable marketing, I make sure they know it takes time. One post will lead to another and then another. Viewers will start by adding you as a friend or even follow you so they can see your next post. Your network is like a tree; it won't grow over night, but the more you nurture it, the bigger it will grow.

A few things that keep your audience intrigued is the amount of energy you show—your positivity, passion, and excitement. Think of it like a movie. The best part is when the climax is about to break: energy/emotions are high and there is suspense, excitement, and a rush! When you have that on your page, it keeps your audience entertained. The more you keep your network open and focus on a variety of viewers, men and women, different races, ages, backgrounds, etc., the more you will start to see more growth.

Most people think in order to be successful with network marketing, you must work all day, every day. Since teaching this kind of marketing, I have seen much more success with working smarter and not harder. I'm working fewer hours a day than ever before and producing ten times the amount than I used to. Not only does this make it more fun, it also makes it more enjoyable and less stressful.

At the end of the day, the people who want to change their lives as much as you do are going to be the successful entrepreneurs. My suggestion: don't chase people. Chasing people can be exhausting, and those that you push to work are going to be the ones that most likely decide not to work. No one really jumps all in until they see the vision and truly focus on where they can go with network marketing. I remember when I first started, I wanted this to work for people so much; I wanted it more for them than they did themselves. It drained me when they didn't put in the effort.

However, there were those select people who were driven and worked without me having to message them constantly. Those are the ones who changed my business 100 percent. Looking back, if there was one thing I wish I knew when I got started, it would be that there are only a small percentage of people who really have the work ethic to be successful.

If you take the leap, just remember that there are a few things that will probably discourage you right away, including the opinions of your families and friends. You may also feel like you don't have enough time or don't know enough people. You may have the impression that you are going to get rich overnight. You may have been told "no" or get turned down immediately or treated negatively. These are all things that you will need to overcome. You need to understand that every single business owner, both inside and outside of network marketing, faces these things. What makes someone truly successful is when they overcome struggles. Think about why you started and remind yourself these struggles are only temporary.

You know you are in the right place when you can write your own schedule, when you don't have to set an alarm clock, don't have to fight traffic, and don't have to report to a boss. There's so much more to experience in life, and network marketing is a door that opens up to a myriad of opportunities, including financial freedom and freedom of time. I now have three kids that know I will always be there for, whether it's attending a school event or cheering them on at one of their sports games. I will never miss these important moments. Freedom of time and never missing a moment are the best feelings! The past can't be changed, but you have the power to change the future.

MOMENTUM MAKERS

1. **BELIEVE IN YOURSELF.** You may not have a single clue about what you're doing, and there are things that may discourage you right away, but stick with it. It takes time but you can overcome these struggles through hard work and determination. Overcoming struggles makes a person truly successful.

2. **LEARN EVERYTHING ABOUT YOUR BUSINESS.** This is a job, so just like in corporate America, learn everything you can about your company and how others in the business have succeeded.

3. **GO AFTER YOUR GOALS AND CRUSH THEM.** Use social media to get people to fall in love with YOU and build a relationship of trust with you before they fall in love with anything you have to offer. Use relatable posts – people and things they can make a connection with on a daily basis. Let people can see the real you.

4. **LIVE THE LIFE YOU HAVE ALWAYS DREAMT OF.** Work smarter, not harder. Life has so much to offer, and network marketing is a door that can open you up to opportunities, financial freedom and time to passionately pursue your dreams and enjoy the life you want!

AMANDA ARNETT

HOT MESS SUCCESS: INTENTION, CONSISTENCY & CONNECTION

I started to write this chapter so many times, and honestly most of those times I just sat here and stared at the blank screen. I was trying to convince myself that I was worthy of such an opportunity to help so many other Network Marketers. Who did I think I was? Why would anyone want to read what this small-town girl from West Virginia had to say? Maybe this stemmed from clear back when one of my teachers in first grade told my mom I was not a good reader. Isn't it funny how those words can stick with us and define us if we let them. Well friends, I am about to share my story with you in the hopes that it will both inspire you and show you that with the right mindset and work ethic you can accomplish anything, no matter what anyone else thinks or says. I will warn you, I tend to type like I talk—I am all over the place—but if you follow along, you will learn a ton, as well as make a new friend, because you were a sport and took time to read all of this. Feel free to add me on Facebook, Instagram and TikTok and let me know if what you read helped you.

My name is Amanda Arnett, and I am from a small town in West Virginia. I grew up knowing that if I wanted to accomplish anything in life, I was going to have to work for it because nothing was going to be given to me. From a young age, I can remember gathering things to sell at yard sales, shoveling snow, raking leaves, having lemonade stands, and basically doing anything and everything to make sure I could afford the things I wanted because I didn't want to ask my parents or anyone else to buy it for me. Like most, I dreamed of one day owning my own home, buying a car, having a career, and a family. However, when I first graduated from high school, I decided to take a year off from school and found out quickly what it was like to work multiple jobs at minimum wage and barely scrape by. I went to cosmetology school for a little while because I could make some extra money on the side doing hair, but that wasn't for me either. So I did what I was always taught in school I should do—I went to college. I originally was a psychology major but my senior year I switched to nursing and sociology, eventually getting a Bachelor of Science and Associates in Nursing degree, collected a ton of debt, and started my career. Along the way, I realized that there was always going to be a limit to what I could do and how much I could make. We truly were struggling to keep up with finances especially with the student loan debt I had accumulated—that was until I was introduced to Network Marketing in the spring of 2013.

So, let me fast forward my story a bit because it's important for you to know where I was when I was introduced to the industry and why I was so open to the idea. Maybe by reading my story you will realize you have many people in your life like myself, that are truly struggling but appear to have it all together. All it took was for the right opportunity at the right time to be presented to me and I was open to hearing it. I remember it like it was yesterday; my husband and I had just come out of one of the hardest years of our lives financially. He had changed jobs to be closer to home and I picked up two jobs as a RN. In one, I was full time on weekend midnights and in the second, I was part time and I would work on days I didn't work at the other hospital. My kids at the time were 2 and 9 so you can imagine how crazy having this schedule was and trying to be a good mommy. I felt guilty constantly for not being home, but eventually my husband found something that was the complete opposite shift as me, and I was able to cut my hours slightly. However, we had gotten so far behind on bills that our car was repossessed in front of our home. I was mortified, sad, scared, and disappointed in how we had let things get so out of control that we lost our car. I knew something had to change at that point, but I didn't know what to do. This was January 2013. I immediately started looking at either going back to school, checking into real estate or something I could do without taking a ton of hours away from my kids. Looking back, I realize I was mentally preparing myself for the opportunity that would come my way just a few months later. Some of you may want to read that again, I WAS TO BE OPEN TO OPPORTUNITIES because I needed something. Many times we present things to people and they just aren't open, so they don't hear us.

I will never forget March 19, 2013, when my mom reached out to me on Facebook and told me I needed to check out what my cousin was doing. Let me first start by telling you I did not know this cousin, and second, I had no clue what network marketing was or how it even worked. I only had 200 friends maybe on Facebook and I had no other social media at the time. I remember shooting her a message asking if all I had to do was share and sell this one product. That's when she explained that I could send people my website and they could order, and it would ship directly to them. In that moment my mind was blown! I didn't know such companies existed, so my next question to her was could I make my money back from my initial investment because honestly, I didn't have much to spare at the time. She explained to me how I could get started, how I could make my money back and how I could share this with others and make a business out of it to make some side money.

In the beginning of my Network marketing career I never imagined making much money, and I believe that is what most other people think as well. However, I knew the possibility had to be there to make some money because she was, and if she was, then I believed I could as well.

Limited beliefs are sometimes instilled at such a young age we don't even realize it, but because of it, I have always approached the business opportunity while introducing it to others as something that is buildable based on effort and what you learn. When you treat your business as a career or education and study it like such, then amazing things can happen. In the first few months of joining the network marketing industry I read a lot of books, listened to a lot of calls, plugged into team pages and chats, and also googled a ton, and still to this day I do the same. As I mentioned previously, I was working a full-time job and a part-time job at the time I joined, so my first goal was how I could quit my part-time job and be home with my kids more. On the one day a week I was home, I would try to set up parties at people's houses or sign up for any event I could get in front of people I didn't know to share my product. Growth was slow and not many were open to the idea. However, I knew from reading, googling and seeing others find success that it was possible for me to achieve success too. That is when I dove headfirst into how I could market online and meet new people, where I could position myself in front of those that would want to use my products and possibly join my opportunity. This decision changed everything for me and eventually led me to earning well over 7 figures in the network marketing industry. I want to make sure it's clear that by no means was I an overnight success and it took a lot of hard work, learning and consistency. Through this journey I have lost my father, retired myself and my husband, collapsed one business and joined another one, fought depression, anxiety, and serious ADHD, and gone through a lot of life changes, all while trying to be the best mother to my two daughters, showing them what is possible. Through it all, even when I have fallen, I have dusted myself off and remembered what this opportunity could do for my family, what it has done for my family and how it could help other families. I hope by reading my story you will see what is possible for you as well, no matter where you are from or what experience you have.

As I continue to share some of the best tips I have in regard to social media, it is very important to realize the platforms are ever changing. You will hear people talk about algorithms and branding and sometimes you'll get distracted. My best advice is to stay focused on your content, being consistent, intentional, and always connecting with new people you would like to get to know more. Also, remember if you are running a business on social media, you are that business, especially in network marketing. Everything you post may attract people to you but just as often may turn people off from you. I tend to stay away from strong political views or responses, and really anything super controversial, however some would completely disagree with that because they do not want to work with people with different views.

I suggest public profiles, but everyone has their own advice on this. My thought process is that if you post something, you want to reach as many people as possible. If you don't want everyone to see what you are posting or your location, especially on Facebook, you can always target and post to only specific friends. However, for the most part, if you are sending out friend requests, you want people to be able to see your page so they know whether they can relate to you or not. When they view your page they should be able to see a variety of who you are and what you are about, not just posts about your products and services.

Let's start with some basics. First and foremost, you do not need to have professional photos by any means, however, you do want to have clean and clear pictures. Good lighting goes a long way also—trust me—that was something I did not do early on and wish I had. The biggest thing on Facebook is that if you are trying to grow your social network on your personal page you need to keep a nice mix of both personal and professional. Remember, no one likes to be sold to and they definitely don't want to be sold to the moment you become friends with them. Try focusing on the long-term goal, which is growing a relationship with that person. Asking yourself why you are friends with them is a good way to make sure you are staying intentional. Likewise, ask yourself these questions: Why would someone want to follow you or friend you on social media? What value do you bring to them? Remember you attract what you are. One simple strategy on Facebook is making sure your personal profile is set up in a way that when someone visits it, they know what you are about. Some examples of my identifiers would be that I am on a weight loss and fitness journey; I had gastric sleeve surgery in 2019; I am a mom of two girls; I am a nurse; I run a business; I am a student; and I love motivating people, making them laugh, and inspiring them daily. When someone comes to my page, that is what they will know me for. It's all about building that know, like and trust factor, as well as true relationships. Not everyone you meet will be part of your business or order your product, and if that is all you are trying to accomplish then you may run into some problems. Building relationships doesn't always mean people will join you, but you better believe they may refer their friends to you if you have something they know may help them. Just like you are not going to order from or join most people you meet; you can't expect everyone else to either.

Some daily actions and ways to add new friends on Facebook would be to start with your hometown, city, and state—people you have met but have never added on your social media platforms. Chances are other friends will have mutual friends with these people and you will show up as familiar, which increases the likelihood of them accepting your request. Make sure your profile picture is clear and of you—a familiar face goes a long way. I love looking up old classmates from elementary all the way through college and reconnecting with them, especially if we were in any type of groups or clubs,. Sharing old pictures and tagging those you are already friends with may also reconnect you with those you are not friends with on social as well. As you continue to do so, you will continue to expand your reach. Another great place to find new friends that you can add to your Facebook are friends you meet in workout classes, parents you meet from your kids' school, or even friends you have met from other social media platforms. I love taking pictures with new friends and asking them if I can tag them on social; this is a great way to both add them and expand your reach in the process. I cannot even tell you how many new friends I have made over the years because someone saw a post I commented on or was tagged in. You can also join groups on Facebook with others that have similar interests as you, but be sure to follow the groups' rules in regard to friending from them, as all groups have their own set of guidelines. Be respectful of that.

Once you make new friends, then what? As I mentioned earlier in this chapter, one of the most important things you can do for your business is get consistent, stay intentional, and always be connecting. I am now going to give you some tips I have learned over the years about posting.

First and foremost, realize that spamming your Facebook with business posts is both against Facebook policy and will annoy your friends to no end. YOU DO NOT WANT EVERYONE TO UNFOLLOW YOU OR BLOCK YOU. So please listen to me on this: Decide daily what your plan is. You can create a baseline example of what you want to post daily. My suggestion is to post something related to business in some way daily no matter what, otherwise always make sure something educates, entertains or inspires. You want to make sure you are connecting with people every day. Be sure to post things that are relevant to you and the people you are adding. What do I mean by that? Well, I wouldn't want to add people that I really have nothing in common with because they wouldn't connect with me and I wouldn't connect with them. Some people prefer to do more attraction marketing and never mention their company or products, however that has never been my approach. I going to leave that decision up to you. I like to think a good mixture keeps things honest, upfront, and approachable, but we all can do this different and still find success, so do what works for you.

Some daily actions you can do aside from posting would be interacting intentionally with peoples' posts and stories. A really easy way to make sure you reach all of your friends even if it's not for business reasons is to start with the letter A and work all the way through the letter Z to intentionally interact on their post and stories. I really love making sure to say happy birthday to people. There are many ways you can do this and my best advice is to not get fancy with it—just focus on being consistent. You can perfect your approach later but most importantly you want to get focused and intentional on actually doing it.

Another great way to interact is to go to your memories on Facebook for on this day and touch base with people that commented on old post or pictures. Sharing these memories is also a great way to spark new conversations with others you may have lost touch with. Again, like I said before, the biggest thing to remember on Facebook is the more love you show others, the more love you will get in return. If your profile does not get a lot of likes and comments, reflect on the content you are providing your audience, who is your audience, and how much are you giving out to them in the process. Before making a post on Facebook, spend a few minutes interacting with your audience, especially those you believe will benefit from what you are about to share. This goes for lives as well. Be sure to comment and love every single post and comment from both your posts and lives. Interacting after the lives or after the post has been posted is another great way to up your reach to those you want to see what you have shared.

Let's move over to some simple strategies for Instagram. From the beginning, I wanted to reach more people then I knew in my community or went to school with. I did not have an Instagram in the beginning of my journey of network marketing. But after researching and realizing the need to expand my network, I decide to use the Instagram platform as my aka Google platform. In theory, the idea I have from this was that if someone was looking for what I had, what did I need to do to position myself to be in front of them. Honestly, that is a good rule of thumb on any platform when going forward in your career as a network marketer.

The use of hashtags is key: utilize them to find your target market, attract your target market and build relationships. As for the right number of hashtags to use, again that's ever changing and debatable. I say stay relevant, and use hashtags that target those that could relate to that specific post. I personally post a set of hashtags in the first comment immediately after making my post In fact, a little tip—right before I hit submit post, I make sure I have my list of hashtags I plan to use so that I can immediately comment them and they will show up most searchable for those looking currently at those specific hashtags.

Creating a strategy will help to really put the utilization of Instagram in place. YOU DO NOT HAVE TO HAVE A PERFECT FEED. Please read that again. While esthetics are important and you do not want to be a slob or come off like you don't care, it is important to remember that everyone starts somewhere. I feel like you attract more people when you are in the beginning stages of building because they can relate to you more versus when you are more established. I recommend a brief description of yourself in your profile as well as links for where they can learn more about your product or services or other social media links. Another tip for you: I created a list from the very beginning focused on specific hashtags that would both relate to me and my products and opportunity. Having a solid list helps to keep people you want to see and that want to see your stuff as a priority, and you want to try to keep it relatively focused and use hashtags surrounding those relatable factors. Daily actions aside from post and stories would be focused on searching hashtags, liking and commenting genuinely on posts and following those that you can relate to and would be possibly be interested in the business or products. DO NOT UNDERESTIMATE COMPLIMENTING BOTH IN STORIES AND IN POSTS—THIS GOES FOR EVERY PLATFORM. Another daily action is going through your personal newsfeed of those you already follow and showing them some loves, and removing those that may not be relevant anymore to what you are trying to accomplish or represent. I like to have a game plan of post, stories, interaction, polls, commenting, liking, new follows, and new searches daily. REMEMBER YOU GET WHAT YOU GIVE.

I also like to recommend connecting your audience (no matter where you met them) to your main platform if possible. I do so by using a landing page link for people to find me on all platforms. Always remember that you can use any method of connection to filter to your main social network.

All social media strategies come down to a few certain things. Staying consistent, being intentional, and connecting to your audience. Everyday, focus on growing your network, your relationships, and yourself. Stay focused on learning new things and always be willing to put yourself out there in the process. Right now, TikTok is a new platform and I have not created a strategy other than how can I expand my reach and what does my audience want from me on there? Did you notice I asked myself what they wanted from me, not how I could get them to join or order? Some may think I am wasting my time; however, I see it as researching and testing my audience for what they want from me. The important thing when a new platform comes around is taking the time to learn and grow with the platform as a marketer. We all remain students for life, especially when it comes to social media and the ever-changing world we live in.

One last tip I would love to give you as we close out this chapter that I hope you forever remember: You can be a Hot Mess and still be a success! You can be all over the place, and not be the best speaker or writer, but if you work hard, continue to learn, show up every single day and put in the work, YOU ABSOLUTLEY CAN BE SUCCESSFUL.

MOMENTUM MAKERS

1. **INTENTION.** What are you doing to continuously group your business day in day out? What is your endgame or ultimate goal with your business? You have to create clear cut goals and a road map to accomplish them and as your vision grows your actions have to meet your expectations of your goals or you will not accomplish them. Long ago someone said do you want to make hobby money or business money? This always stuck with me because even though it may seem like pennys at first remember Rome wasn't built in a day and you have to build the momentum in any business to achieve greatness.

2. **CONNECTION.** How are you expanding your network on a daily basis and what value are you bringing to that network? Continue to find people to connect with in some way shape or form and continue to build on that. Whether that connection leads into a friendship, referral or business potential at the end of the day the relationship has to remain the most important focus.

3. **CONSISTENCY.** What actions are you doing day in and day out to achieve what you want? Mindless scrolling on social media, never communicating or building your skills, not plugging in, not learning from others and applying a clear plan will have you spinning in circles. I suggest a short power hour burst where you have a list you pound out of intentional actions daily. That can be anything you want it to be but you want to stick to mainly income producing activities you do not have to rely on a response to keep going.

4. **EVERYDAY.** Learn something NEW everyday!

5. **MINDSET.** Your mindset is going to determine everything.

BRIAN FRYER

FROM PRO BASEBALL

I'm just an average guy who grew up in Southern California, loves the beach, and dreamed of one day playing professional baseball . . .

Network marketing was never really on my radar, but I'm so thankful my mind was opened. It has forever changed my life.

My name is Brian Fryer, and I'm a 12-year Network Marketing veteran who loves all things network marketing, business, and social media! Although I have now mentored tens of thousands of people on how to grow their businesses online, some things weren't always so simple!

In summer 2008, I had been a professional baseball player for almost four years. I was home for the off-season in Ventura, CA working an oil-field job (because, let's be honest, minor league baseball salary was nothing to get excited over) and was working out as much as possible to stay in shape. Although I was working 50-60 hours a week, I still found time every day to hit the gym and/or head to the local junior college where I once played to hit some baseballs and stay fresh.

Doing my best to stay in shape, putting on some muscle, and working to attain peak performance, I did something that would stay with me the rest of my life.

While lifting weights at the local L.A. Fitness gym one afternoon, I took it a bit too far. I was doing squats near the end of a workout and something terrible happened. As I squatted down nearing one of the last few reps, I could not get back up; I had thrown my back out. My lower back had completely shifted, and I immediately knew this was NOT going to be good.

Bed-ridden for the next few days with icing and lots of ibuprofen, I was praying it would not affect my baseball career.

I spent the next couple of months at the doctor's office, multiple massage therapists, and even the chiropractor, and it was still not getting much better. At this point, I was actually starting to panic a little knowing the upcoming baseball season was fast-approaching, and I didn't know if I would be ready to go by then.

I then ran into a great family friend who asked how my back was doing and proceeded to bring up that a friend of hers also had some back issues and starting drinking some miracle juice and that I should try it.

Of course, I was skeptical, but at that point was willing to do ANYTHING to help my back recover before the next baseball season. Within a week, I met up with this guy and tasted the product. He gifted me the bottle, and I drank it religiously for the next seven days. To save you the play-by-play, within those seven days I felt almost back to 100% . . . I was SHOCKED! I gave this guy a call and shared my testimony in amazement. He acted as if he "expected" my response to be that and was really excited for me. Naturally, after I began asking a few more questions about how to order my own, he invited me to learn a bit more about this product and the possibility of making a few extra bucks by sharing it with others.

Now remember, I was making decent money in the oil-field working VERY hard for the six months I was home during the off-season, but knowing I was headed back to spring training soon and that the minor-league salary was nothing to rave about, I knew every little bit of extra money would help. But I was not the LEAST BIT interested in "selling" anything. See, I had this master plan of believing my then girlfriend, Dani (and now wife), would be GREAT at selling it, ha!

That next week at the beautiful Crowne Plaza hotel in Ventura, CA, I attended my FIRST network marketing meeting with over 200 people in this standing-room-only event, in which everyone was buzzing, excited, and smiling! The energy in that room was incredible. I had NO IDEA what I was in for, what I would soon learn, or how this one moment would forever change my life.

We actively built with this company for the next four years WITHOUT making a single dollar in profit. Now let me explain . . . we made money, but between our auto-ship each month, the three events we traveled to each year, and all the swag and business-building materials, we did not technically MAKE any money. I can remember each year talking with our tax advisor and claiming a LOSS for the business each year.

To be honest, my mind was elsewhere with finishing up my baseball career and was simply NOT open to learning about and refining the skill-sets necessary to actually build this type of business. The light bulb still had NOT clicked on for me. During those four years I turned into that annoying friend and family member who wouldn't shut up about my product and business that was going to change everybody's life, yet they were all still waiting for me to even get any results.

This was also a VERY difficult time because when it came to all the meetings, we had to either drag our toddler around with us or spend the evening apart because Dani would have to stay home with her. This happened far too often and was very tough after working all day and then not being with my family in the evening. On top of that, trying to talk our warm market into this after seeing us sacrifice was a tough sell.

To put this in perspective, I was that ANNOYING person on social media who was trying to convince all their friends to buy his product and why my business was what they needed. I fell into the trap of trying to convince everyone for four straight years . . . and it didn't work.

We would literally go to family functions and the room full of people would SCATTER as we walked in. Why? Because they were all fearful that we would eventually try to get them in our business or buy our overpriced product. Needless to say, we ran through our warm market and NONE of them joined us.

Can you relate?

Have you run through your warm market and are now sitting there wondering if you can even be successful now?

Have you thought that if your family won't join, why would anyone else join you?

My hope is that through the rest of our story you realize YOU can do this. What one person can do, so can another. Whether all of your family members and friends join you or not, YOU can achieve any amount of success that you desire, but it's gonna take grit, hard work, and resilience. You are guaranteed to experience challenges, obstacles, critics, ups & downs, and (yes) wins of all kinds. There are people in this amazing profession who have come from much more difficult situations than the one maybe you are in right now, but they persevered and not only made it through to the other side but have made a PROFOUND impact on the lives of so many others.

Unfortunately after four years with that first company, they were merging with another. Although this was tough to swallow, we decided to move on and go our own way. My wife actually decided to "take a break" from network marketing because we had run off all of our family members and friends, and she wanted to work on restoring those relationships. Now while I wanted to do that too, I knew in my SOUL that this profession could change our lives—I just had to figure out HOW.

So while she went one direction (sitting on the sidelines), I stayed in the game. I literally hopped in the car, drove down to Best Buy and bought myself a laptop. Why? Because we had run off anyone and everyone who was remotely close to us, and I needed to figure out how to meet some NEW people. At that time, there was some BUZZ and talk about this cool new platform on the Internet called "The Facebook."

I figured, what the heck, nothing to lose! This will give me an opportunity to not only make some new friends but also make a brand new first impression with these people every single day!

For the next two years, I invested in courses, coaching, and programs and did a LOT of implementing a messing up. I dabbled with a couple of tech companies in the network marketing space, developed a little footprint with minimal success, and actually made a few bucks. During this time, though, I was testing, trying, and learning how this new thing called "social media" could work to my advantage in building a business not only in my state or in my country but also around the world. That whole thought of eventually making money while I slept was FASCINATING to me, and I knew that network marketing was the vehicle that could help me create something like this. I'm an introvert at heart, and the thought of doing home meetings terrified the you-know-what out of me.

With one daughter at the time and knowing Dani and I wanted a much bigger family eventually and that I didn't have too many more years playing baseball left, I was thinking long term.

What would I do for work? How would I make an income? How could we eventually work from home, make good money, help people, and OWN our time?

I knew I didn't want to work in the oil field forever, and just felt it DEEP in my soul that this vehicle of network marketing could fulfill these dreams. I wasn't scared of doing the work . . . heck I worked my tail off my whole life with the aspiration of playing professional baseball!

Seven years into network marketing we still had not seen any significant or life-changing success, but we were making progress. After a few of those tech opportunities fell through, we prayed for something that aligned with our core values and beliefs and would allow us to make the biggest impact possible.

A few months after that, I received a message from a mentor who had made over nine million dollars in network marketing, so to say I was listening intently was an understatement. There was a brand new company launching that promoted toxic-free and organic products. Now that we had two daughters and were consciously making better decisions about the products we were bringing in our home, we were all ears!

We had already been sharing the benefits of getting rid of the chemical-laden products in our home with our friends and family for the previous eight months and thought this would be simple to share something that came naturally.

As I approached Dani about this phone call, she told me that she was only open to building alongside of me if we COMMITTED to doing things a little differently than the norm. Knowing what we had personally gone through our first four years and hardly ever seeing my wife and daughter, there was NO WAY we were going to ask other families to do this. We wanted to teach people how they could leverage social media so they could TRULY work from home. We were going to focus on EDUCATION and not just try to slam-dunk everyone we could into a business. Our hearts were in educating, genuinely helping and allowing families, especially those with kids, to see the reality and harmful effects of products with harsh chemicals in their homes and what the ramifications could be.

Although Dani was still technically on the sidelines, this is something she was SO EXCITED about and confident we could do well, building this together. This was a pivotal moment for me because I felt like I had my partner back and we were going to do this together.

What was our secret to success?

We didn't try to SELL our products or convince people why they needed them.

We simply educated them on the harmful effects of what they may be currently using, which led them to asking us what we used and recommended. This was so much more fun than chasing people around fielding all the pyramid question talk.

We may have been seen as the "Black Sheep" at first with this new company because we were the ONLY ones building online and were NOT interested in doing home meetings, but their thoughts quickly changed about us just six months into building this business as we sky-rocketed to become the #4 earners, working it 100% online. Now don't get me wrong—we believe wholeheartedly that home meetings and 3-ways calls work. It just didn't fit how WE wanted to build. With two young daughters, a full-time job and as a baseball coach to a travel baseball team for twelve year olds, I wanted to put to use all I had been learning the previous few years.

Over the next two and a half years, we experienced the trips, bonuses, recognition, and blessings that come with being a top earner, but unfortunately that all went away when the company decided to merge with another that didn't align with our values and core beliefs. We were stuck in the middle of a rock and hard spot. Do we go seek another company to join, or was there something God was calling us to do?

Over the course of the next few weeks as we were trying to make sense of this all, I received dozens of emails, messages, and phone calls from leaders all around the world, all different companies asking if I could teach them what we had just done on social media and, more importantly, help their team.

This was my confirmation to step into the mentoring and coaching space, knowing our track record, our story, and what we were able to create because we DID it ourselves. I felt the impact we could make would help and serve even more than the thousands who were on our team because I would now be coming from a generic perspective, not affiliated with a specific company. The daily activities, the systems and processes, the team building and duplication secrets, and building a personal & professional brand online that led us to enrolling over 700 people would be the basis from which I could bless so many more people.

Over the last five years, we've been blessed to train tens of thousands of network marketers and entrepreneurs on how to build a business the right way online through our Virtual Impact Academy program as well as personally mentor hundreds as one-on-one clients. Although my approach may sound a little different from what you may be used to hearing, it still focuses on the CORE fundamentals of building a successful business—value, relationships, being authentic, and understanding how you can make an even BIGGER impact through your business and not just focused on a title or rank.

The question now becomes . . . how can I help you?

Below are a couple of my BEST tips to helping you grow your name, brand and business online.

1. Your name is your brand. Every post, comment, or video you make has YOUR NAME attached to it. Whether it's good (or bad), it will reflect your brand. Why is establishing YOUR NAME so critical in my opinion? Well that's simple to understand: you are NOT in the products business or whose comp plan is better business; you are in the PEOPLE business—don't you ever forget that. If people don't know, love, or trust you, they will NEVER buy from you, let alone join you in business. Social media (heck, business in general) isn't about how you can sell more products. Rather it is about how you can EARN the trust of more people. If they trust you, they will buy from you and consider doing business with you. This is how we went from enrolling fifty people personally over the first seven years of our career to enrolling over 700 the last three. The question you must answer is: Do you want to blend in with the other 1,000/10,000/100,000 reps in your company online or do you want to STAND OUT? I'm sure this answer is unanimously to stand out.

2. LIVE video could be your ticket to freedom. After doing over 2,500 LIVE videos now myself, I've realized some really cool things. I'm an introvert, and the thought of speaking in front of people or doing LIVE videos has bothered me since I was in college, yet it is something I'm working to get better at each day. Given I've already had half a dozen speaking gigs presented to me already just this year, I believe it's God's way of showing me how to continue stepping outside of my comfort zone. Although LIVE video can be powerful, what we've realized is so many have no clue how or why to use them. A simple formula we've used that has helped our clients generate tens of millions in commissions is as follows: Title, Intro, Hook, Content, CTA (call to action).

We suggest starting with THREE areas of focus for content. One should be related to YOUR niche of business (a.k.a. health and wellness, skincare, clean products, service, etc.), and the other two should be areas of interest/hobbies you can provide value around to HELP that particular community of people. We encourage you to do three or four PUBLIC live videos per week. A BONUS tip: Keep them 5-7 minutes long. Everyone is BUSY and has squirrel syndrome. Keep them short, sweet, and to the point, engage with your viewers, smile, and have fun. If you have an entertaining or funny bone in your body, this always warms up the crowd that much sooner. As for your "business-type" live videos, we never suggest mentioning your product or company name, and this is key.

3. If you want to receive, you must GIVE first! The social media code is pretty simple to crack. If you want more comments on your posts, go comment on others' posts more often! If you want more LIVE viewers on your video, go tune in and engage on others' videos! If you want more people reaching out to you, YOU should be focused on reaching out to others to genuinely connect. It's pretty simple, yet so many miss this SIMPLE strategy when it comes to building online. They expect to make a post and sell a bunch of stuff. They make a family post and expect EVERYONE to like and comment on it. What's one simple thing you can focus on with this thought? GIVE through the content you are posting! Posts, videos, stories, and comments, are ALL opportunities for you to GIVE to others! Whether it's a laugh or three helpful tips to live a more balanced life, there are people out there STARVING for the information you haven't shared yet. GIVE it to them! The more you are willing to give, the more TRUST you will earn and, well, we now know how that typically goes, don't we?

No matter how many friends or followers you have, no matter your rank or level of income, and no matter how long you have STRUGGLED in this amazing profession, YOU can create any level of success you desire if you'll CHOOSE to use social media the right way. The opportunity awaits you. The question is now if you are open and willing to listen, learn and implement consistently. If you are, you will positively impact a whole lot of people. It's not about trying to become an "influencer"; it's about becoming a person of impact! If you'll focus on impact, the money and all the other cool stuff will follow. God bless you, your family, and your business.

MOMENTUM MAKERS

1. **BRAND YOURSELF!** You have to make a decision of whether you want to STAND OUT online, or blend in with everyone else!

2. **GO LIVE!** It's the fastest, simplest and most efficient way to get your name, and content out into the marketplace!

3. **GIVE MORE!** If "giving" is our focus, this comes from a place of servitude! When we serve, we earn trust! Trust opens the door for more opportunities to share your product and business!

4. **BE AUTHENTIC!** God made you perfect in His image! Don't be afraid of being yourself. Your story will inspire many!

5. **FOCUS ON IMPACT, NOT INFLUENCE!** The number of followers or friends you have online is irrelevant. Focus on making a difference and the money will follow!

DJ BARTON
THE "MOBILEPRENEUR" LIFE

I want to set the stage for you to have the best success you deserve in our amazing profession. So many people always wonder, "Can I actually do this?" The short answer is, "Yes, you can." The real question should be, "Do I have the true desire to have more in life than I currently have right now?" If you answered yes, then you have exactly what it takes. It does have to be followed up by consistent action, though. In life, thoughts determine what you want, and action determines what you get.

I was introduced to network marketing at the age of 18 years old. I'd never done anything like this, nor had I ever heard of this profession. I grew up in a small town in Minnesota. Let's just say I had a not so normal up bringing. In this day in age, is there even such a thing as normal, anyways? Yes, I was loved, I had friends and all the normal stuff, like food on the table, etc. I grew up middle class. Not wealthy not poor. I did not get a lot of extras, however I had what I thought was enough. Something tragic did happen, though, a month before my 8th birthday that forever, and still to this day, changed my life. I believe lots of my drive for success and better quality of life comes from this tragedy. I lost my hero, the man I looked up to in many ways—my dad. He was killed accidently in a plane crash, and I never had the pleasure of seeing him again. From that day forward, consciously or subconsciously, I always had a different outlook on life.

I grew up for the most part in a single parent home with a mother who was absolutely perfect in my eyes. She tried to find love; men were in and out of my life. I learned some great lessons from them and her: things to do and definitely what not to do, and lots of life lessons along the way. I grew up faster then most, mindset wise. I always had a great work ethic; I was hungry to make money and have success. I have a secret to tell you. I rode the struggle bus in school bad! I got along great with my teachers and kids, etc., but I was the worst student you could imagine. I had bad comprehension—I would read a book and forget all that I had read. "Why?" you may ask. Daydreaming is what I called it. Lack of motivation and interest is more than likely what my teachers and my mom called it. Long story short, let's just say I learned young and before the rest that school was not my deal.

I got my first job at 13 and was more than excited to have my own money coming in. From age 13 to 18, I had so many fun jobs that allowed me to make money and to have my own independence young and fast. I had my own snowmobiles at 15, trucks at 16, and I moved out when I was 18. Mom was a little mad that I moved out at 18 about four months before I finished high school. It was not far; it was across the lake. However, for the first time, I tasted FREEDOM! I learned that freedom was my new action motivator going forward in life.

I knew two things when I turned 18. One, I was not interested in going to college. To please my mom, I did go to take a placement test at a 2-year community college. While taking the test that tells you what you would be good at for school, I asked where the restroom was and never returned. That's as close as I got. Let's just say mom was not excited about that at that point in time. The second thing I knew was that getting a job was not going to fulfill my dreams and goals in life… especially in the small town I was raised in. So, along with two of my great friends at the time, I said, "Why don't we move to Phoenix, Arizona, and go make our dreams come true?" We figured big city big ideas, warm weather and no snow—perfect! Within months, we all moved to Phoenix to chase our dreams, and we found a place to live and call home.

All three of us started looking for jobs to get us on our feet. I really did not want a job; I found an ad in the paper that said, "We will pay you to go to real estate school." I thought, "Hmm… my grandfather and my dad were very successful in real estate. Grandpa retired at 50, and Dad was on track until the accident." I thought, "Why not follow the footsteps and carry on the legacy?" Plus, this ad said they would pay for it. Getting paid to go to school for something you had a genuine interest in is a little different than paying to go to a school you have zero interest in. So, I got the deal within days of being in Phoenix. As for my two friends, they had a little different story. However this was again a turning point in my career. A MAJOR turning point. (PS… I say career, but I did not really have a career—I was just in real estate school. I thought it was my career though.)

Weeks went by and my friends circled ad after ad, and they finally had a breakthrough. They called about a sales and marketing ad at the time. I forgot which one of them called, but they both went to the interview together. The guy on the phone said, "Bring your friend; we are expanding rapidly." After real estate school for that day, after only a few weeks in, I went back to the apartment we were living in, and I saw them having a blast on our patio listening to music and have gin and juice. I thought, "What happened today at the interview?" They said, "We found it." "You found what?" "We found a way we will make lots of money and be rich." I said, "OK, how are we going to be rich and make lots of money?" In the back of my mind I was also wondering how they were able to get the gin and juice at our age. But that was beside the point. This was on a Tuesday night. They really could not explain what they saw. They did say it was too much to explain and were saying how we are going to make lots of money selling water filters and health products. I laughed and said, "OK. What do we know about any of this?" They said they didn't, but they will teach us. I asked, "Who are they?" "The people we met at the meeting." They tried to explain about the meeting but I did not really get it. I honestly thought they got brainwashed. They said, "You should come down on Thursday and see what we saw." In the back of my mind I was thinking "See what you saw? You have both lost it." "I'll go down to tell them you are not interested and then back off to real estate school for me." Let's just say that didn't end the way I imagined it would.

I went to the meeting with them. They dressed up, which I thought was weird in itself. Business attire. I went into a group interview with about 100 people. The energy was electric for an interview. I met tons of excited, upbeat, positive people. I sat there very quietly and just listened. I'm an introvert unless I'm in my element—my now network marketing element. The presentation was about an hour. I saw the products, and I saw the compensation plan. None of it made sense to me, really, other than the fact you can make lots of money. What the hook was for me was the fact that you could write your own paycheck—the harder you worked, the more you could make. No qualifications, no college degrees needed, no nothing. Only heart and desire along with work ethic. I was thinking to myself, "I got this." Then at the end of the presentation they showed a testimonial reel. One testimony stood out to me the most. It was a guy: dark hair and successful, sitting at his pool in the back yard, with a Mercedes in the front of a big nice home. It was as if he was talking directly to me. He talked about following a system, being coachable, plugging into the leadership and mentorship. He had a weird resemblance to what my dad looked like prior to his passing, and I became very good friends with him over time. I worked hard to gain his respect and attention; in this business you work where you are deserved, not needed. That was a little different than what I was used to. However, he became the father figure and roll model I never had. To this day we are still great friends and talk often.

So let's talk business. For the record, I had NO business even being in this business. I think that is what motivated me the most. People looked at me different. What was this 18-year-old kid going to teach me? In my mind I thought, "Nothing, haha. I'm going to introduce you to the right people who will teach you."

Our profession is a lot different today than it was 24 years ago when I first joined network marketing. I know we are never supposed to say what we do is easy… because it's not. The work and systems and finding people is easy. The game you play in your mind is what makes it hard. I can say it's easier than it has ever been. When I first started in our profession, I had to pay for and run ads to find people looking for work. We didn't have a resume' system—we had to grab the good ole phone book and smile and dial. We would go to the mall and compliment people on how great their shoes, watch, clothes, etc. looked and start conversations. We would go to networking events to meet business professionals. I would even put on roller blades after 10pm and go to the parked cars at airports and put flyers on the windshields. Why did I do all this, you may ask? Well, when I started, they told me to go to people who know, like and trust you. I did that… family, friends, and co-workers while I was growing up. They all knew, liked and trusted me, but they did not look up to me when it came to business. I signed up less than 10 people that I knew. Plus, most of them all thought I was in some pyramid scheme. In my mind I knew I was right and they were wrong. Whenever people gave me negative objections, it really just fueled my fire inside to go work harder. I said one of us would be right. I was not going to fail at that point, no matter what. So I went after it hard, with consistent effort, and over time it worked for me. I got lots of objections rejections, and tons of "no's", but that did not stop me. If anything, it confused me. I believe that our industry is the greatest opportunity on the planet. No limitations: you can be from jail or Yale, and come from a poor or rich background. Just shoot for the stars. The scary part is, after 22 years into my journey, I almost quit. Yup, you heard it. What I have learned is that almost every leader will tell you (if they are being honest) that they almost quit, too. Now, would I really quit? No! I just thought of quitting. We all ride the emotional roller coaster. The key is to stay buckled and hold on until the ride is over. For me, I can never see the ride being over. I LOVE what I do. When you love what you do, you will truly never work a day in your life.

Three rules I learned that will help you.

1. Pay attention

2. Get excited.

3. Never quit.

If you follow these rules you will make it. I could go into an entire training on this topic alone, but that is for another time.

I want to talk to you about what changed my business and kept me going, I believe this will help you get to the top of your goals like it's helped me. The reason I thought about quitting was because I got burnt out. I was selling the dream of freedom, which is my number one motivator in life. When you make $1 dollar more in residual income then your residual bills, to me that is freedom. But I felt like I was living a lie. I was doing 1-on-1 and 2-on-1 meetings from 8am-5pm at coffee shops every day. I was doing home meetings almost every night. When I was not doing those in my city, I was traveling to a team member's town to do the same thing. I really was time broke, which was not what I called freedom. Don't get me wrong; it is fun for a while. However, we are in the home-based business profession. I want to be home or building on my terms from anywhere around the world. Remember freedom? Work when you want, with whom you want, where you want. Who doesn't want that? I know you do.

I wasn't leveraging technology and social media like I should or could at the time. In December of 2017, I started seeing lots of my friends in our profession leveraging social media like I had never seen before. What I really saw was they were working less and making more. But more importantly, they had their time back. That is when I had the idea of becoming a "Mobilepreneur"—being able to leverage social media in so many ways. As long as you have a Wi-Fi connection, you are in business. For me that meant no more meetings in coffee shops and living rooms… total time freedom.

I started becoming a student all over again. I reached out to my friends and asked lots of question, and took a bunch of notes, as if it was my first training all over again. I really was inspired. No boundaries to your business. As long as your company is in that country you can do business. It's never been so fun and simple to grow and connect with anyone. You're just one click away from your next relationship.

I'm going to share a few nuggets that helped me along the way that I know will help you as well. Yes, your image is everything. I'll let you think about that for a minute. Would you work with you? Would you recruit you? If the answer is not what you're looking for, you need to make some changes.

What I want to talk to you about is hunting and fishing. Yes, that is right, you heard it correctly. There are two major ways you can generate leads online. Before I start, I want you to fall in love with the process and fall in love with the activity. The results will come over time.

Let's talk hunting first. Hunting is when you go on social media and direct message (DM) people to see if they are open to your product, service or opportunity. Side note: there are many great scripts out there you can use. I want you to understand the concept first. The DM works on all platforms of social media. Don't overthink this step. Pick one that resonates with you the most. If you're more business savvy, you might like Linkedin; if you're younger, you may prefer Instagram, Snapchat, TikTok or ding dong. (Ding dong is not really a thing.) If you are in the middle, you may prefer Facebook. Pick one platform to start. It's hard to be in a boat with six fishing lines in the water trying to catch fish. Pick 1-2 fishing spots at a time, perfect those, then scale up.

When I started, I built my Facebook list up first. I did not overthink this. I printed my Facebook list (ask Google how), and I went from A-Z asking everyone if they were open to taking a look at what I had to offer. I made it a game in my head… I looked at it as if I was cleaning out my contacts and seeing who I was connected with. Once I went through my direct contacts, I started looking for groups and pages that I would have something in common with the people in those groups. For example, if you are a single mom, go to single mom groups or if you like corvettes, go into corvette groups. Find some local groups in your area and larger groups. Make sure that the groups are active and have posts daily. (Make sure you follow the group rules.) Remember, this is social media. BE social. Go in the groups and add value: like and comment on people's posts to be seen. Comment on people's comments about other people's comments. We live in a weird world. You can take a cold market and bring them to a warm market quickly if you like.

Want me to share a secret with you? The more you engage on posts, the more people see your name. The more they see your name, psychologically you get embedded in their brain and when you reach out it's like they already know you. I'll give you one of my favorite examples. Pick a group—the page does not matter. Remember, people like to do business with people like them. Find a group you would find yourself being in. Go find posts that have comments and likes on them. Find comments in these groups that are good comments.

Step 1—Like the comment

Step 2—Comment on someone's comment that added value. For example, comment "Spot on," "Thank you for this, "or "Great comment."—Write something that you would say. Then I go to that person's profile and send them a friend request along with sending them a message that says: "Great value add on that post. Where are you from?" I then wait for them to reply and start a conversation and compliment them. I follow this with an invite.

There are 2 billion plus people on social media, so don't worry, there are plenty of fish in the water.

Places you can find unlimited fish (prospects) in:

- Groups (Facebook, Linkedin)

- Facebook pages

- Friends of friends with common interests

- Sponsored ads (Not your sponsored ads, I'm talking other people's ads. The ads that show up on your feeds typically are interests that you have. That means other people similar to you. Like, share and comment on them. Apply the same hunting skills that you just learned above here, too.)

- Instagram (You can follow influencers and specific hashtags that you are interested in and that would be beneficial for your business.)

With just this hunting skill alone you can build an empire.

Now let's talk more about fishing. There are many ways to fish with social media. Fishing is when they come to you because you attracted them to you. This is also known as "Attraction Marketing."

There are many ways that you can attract leads to you. Before I dive into it, one of the things you really want to understand is to not be one dimensional with your posting topics. Post topics you have true interest in. Remember, like attracts like.

Examples of topics:

- Facebook Lives (Most powerful)

- Family

- Travel/Lifestyle/Fun

- Personal development

- Entrepreneurship

- Inspirational

Your goal is to create engagement (Likes, Shares and Comments). Ask questions so there is lots of dialog on your page.

Don't over post. What does that mean? You need to have the algorithms work with you, not against you. When it comes to stories on Facebook and Instagram, you can post and document your daily life… there is no limit. This is where the world wants to see the real you. Be vulnerable, authentic and natural. People don't like fake people. When it comes to your news feed, I recommend only posting 1-2 times a day and least 4-6 hours a part. You don't want your post to fight for attention. I do recommend posting every day. Look at it like your TV channel; it never is blank is it? So, don't let your profile be blank. Your goal is to consistently add value.

When posting on social media, include "curiosity posts." Recognize rank ups and testimonials of people in your business (without saying the full name of the person or the name of the company). Curiosity kills the cat—if they can go to your profile and google what you post and find out what you do, then you lose.

When it comes to story posts, this is by far the future of social media. You can ask questions with all the benefits and features to create engagement. Some work better than others; just find your rhythm and what works best for you.

Another great way to generate leads, which is one of the best, is referral posts. You will run into people that say, "I don't know anyone." LOL, first of all, that is a crock of crap if we are being honest. What they are saying is, "I'm not sure I believe in myself and if I have what it takes or not." They have limited belief and self-doubts. So, your job is to build them up and help them WIN. That's my rant, now let's get back to business.

The referral post is so powerful. This is when you reach out to people on social media that you are connected with and ask if they would be willing to put a post on their wall using a curiosity post, and they tag you in it. You have to coach them on what to say if people reach out to them in a DM. This is great because now you can build through your networks contacts and get them regardless of whether they are in your business or not. I use this tool for fence sitters—people that are just not interested and have said NO. I always get a referral post. You can get the No's fishing for you. With fence sitters and the No's, you can get them to say yes once you get someone in their network interested. FOMO kicks in. I also use it as an indirect approach to show my network.

Example Scripts:

"Hey John, I'm really focused and productive with my online business right now. I don't think what I do would be a fit for you, but would you be open to doing a referral post for me?" (Explain what it is, send an example and set up the expectations.) In my mind I'm thinking, "How would they know if it is or isn't a fit? What is it?" Bam, you got them to look.

Example Scripts:

"Hey John, I'm super excited about a business I am working on part time online. I know you have tons of connections on social, so would you be willing to do me a huge favor? It would mean the world to me!" (Explain what a Referral post is, etc.) Then suggest, "Why don't I show you what I am doing so if one of your contacts reach out to you, you can validate that I've got the real deal going on." Now you have another exposure.

I can assure you that with the information you learned in this chapter along with all the other great knowledge in other chapters, you could be dropped out of a plane (with a parachute of course) and be successful anywhere around the world. All I want to do is impact one person and it was worth it.

I'm going to leave you with one last nugget to tie this all together. You must have a DMO (Daily Method Of Operation). It does not matter if you are working your business part time or full time. Set your activity goals and track your daily numbers.

DMO:

- How many new DMs a day?

- How many follow ups a day?

- How many presentations a day?

- Did you do your curiosity posts?

- How many referral posts a day?

- Did you read a chapter in a book?

- Did you listen to an audio for 15 min?

- Did you do your lives?

What you track gets measured, and what gets measured, you can improve on. You must have fun and just get started. You can't wait for the perfect time to start. You just have to start. Go -> Set -> Ready. If we wait until we're ready, we'll be waiting the rest of our life. The biggest commodity in life is time. We don't know how much of it we have. The other is attention—eyes on us. Think about this. You could be the worst network marketer but outearn the best network marketer. Why you ask? It's simple: you just have to be the most impactful social presence and marketer to drive traffic to your presentation. The most eyes on you wins.

This is the new era of our amazing profession, so don't get caught in the old ways or you will be left behind. Follow your heart and live your life with passion. Most importantly, have FUN!! We are in the fun business, making your dreams into reality.

Due to Social Media Marketing along with all the amazing tools, systems and leadership, I am able to build a global business from my smartphone and be a true Mobilepreneur. You can too!

———— MOMENTUM MAKERS ————

1. **YOU HAVE WHAT IT TAKES TO BE SUCCESSFUL IN NETWORK MARKETING.** If you have a true desire to have more in life, and are willing to follow it up by consistent actions and hard work, you will succeed. Follow a system, be coachable, and plug into the leadership of your company for mentoring. Set activity goals and track your daily numbers.

2. **WHEN YOU LOVE WHAT YOU DO, YOU WILL TRULY NEVER WORK A DAY IN YOUR LIFE.** We all ride the emotional roller coaster and have days when we want to jump off. The key is to stay buckled in and hold on until the ride is over (or stay on it forever)!

3. **UTILIZE DIRECT MESSAGING (DM).** Using whichever social media platform you're comfortable with, DM people to see if they are open to your product, service or opportunity.

4. **FIND GROUPS AND PAGES THAT YOU HAVE INTERESTS IN COMMON WITH THE PEOPLE IN THOSE GROUPS.** Find local groups and larger groups. Make sure they are active and people are posting in them daily. BE SOCIAL AND ADD VALUE! Like and comment on posts to be seen.

5. **THE MORE YOU ENGAGE ON POSTS, THE MORE PEOPLE SEE YOUR NAME.** The more they see your name, psychologically, you get embedded in their brain, and when you reach out to them, it's like they already know you.

— **MOMENTUM MAKERS** —

6. **ATTRACT LEADS TO YOU USING "ATTRACTION MARKETING".** On your page, post topics you have true interest in, like Facebook Lives, family, travel, personal development, inspirational topics, etc. Your goal is to create engagement. Give enough information to encourage someone's curiosity, but not enough that they can google you and see what you do.

7. **ASK FOR REFERRAL POSTS.** Reach out to people on social media that you are connected with and ask if they would be willing to put a post on their wall/page using a curiosity post, and tag you in it. This is great because now you can build through your networks contacts and get them regardless of whether they are in your business or not.!

CPSIA information can be obtained
at www.ICGtesting.com
Printed in the USA
LVHW021332160221
679326LV00005B/734

9 781628 658064